Out of the Fog

Out of the Fog

Meditations For
Believers and Skeptics

*To Brooks,
with gratitude
for all you are
and do,
Sarah*

Sarah Clark

To order additional copies of this book, contact:
Xlibris Corporation
1-888-795-4274
www.Xlibris.com
Orders@Xlibris.com
43957

Contents

DEDICATION

*This book is dedicated to the congregations I have served in
Plymouth, Massachusetts, Peterborough, New Hampshire, Kenosha, Wisconsin,
Rochester, New York, West Roxbury, Massachusetts, East Boston, Massachusetts,
The Church of the Larger Fellowship, Boston, Massachusetts and
to the church which ordained me, thus starting me on this writing journey,
The Independent Christian Church, Unitarian Universalist
in Gloucester, Massachusetts,
and most especially, to my friends and fellow writers,
Ingeborg Lauterstein and Lois Reed, who encouraged me from Day One,
And, of course, to Aram, Hans and Alex Schwartz,
who provide me with endless inspiration.*

Out of the Fog

One summer morning in Castine, Maine, the fog played tricks. One moment we saw a beautiful four-masted ship in the harbor; the next, only a spectral gray haze. The ship was as invisible as if it had ceased to exist. Yet, we knew that somewhere in the mist, she was anchored securely.

Soon we saw a dory emerge from the curtain of gray. Its crew of summer sailors rowed to the dock with buoyant smiles, happy to have gone to sea, happy to be ashore. What were the stories they shared with friends on land? Did they tell of stars on midnight wave, dolphins leaping in the sun? Feeling the earth solid beneath their feet, did they long for the movement of the ocean, the sense of being clasped by a great and powerful force, rocked as the old hymnist wrote, "in the cradle of the deep"?

Did they look back into the fog at the cloud-cloaked ship and wonder at the mystery of the seen and the unseen, the ship disappearing and reappearing as the fog rolled and listed over the bay? Were they reminded of the eternal rocking of our planet spinning through space? Did they realize that, whether on land or sea, we are eternally rocked and swirled and spun by a great and phenomenal force, gravity, thermodynamics, god, goddess, nature, call it what we will?

The mystery of that force is obscured by the fog of our everyday lives, yet there are those rare moments when the fog lifts, and we see—briefly and exquisitely—the unseen, when we are one with the heartbeat of the universe.

The summer sailors disembarked cheerily and made a beeline for the coffee shack and then up the street in search of news of civilization, whether in the form of *The Wall Street Journal,* a call to their broker, or a long lunch with earthbound friends over lobsters at the village inn. This was, after all, Castine, where the following conversation was overheard in a local shop:

"How does your granddad like his new Volvo? Doesn't he miss the Mercedes?"

"I don't know about him. I miss it. But it would take a year to get a Mercedes with all-wheel drive. He said winters in Maine that's more important."

Castine is a town of privilege and of practicality. It is the Maine of rich summer visitors and retirees, with, I would guess, only a smattering of the original natives proudly driving pick-up trucks or sedans that have seen better days and hanging on to the homes they love with the tenacity of barnacles on rock.

Perhaps Castine is not so unlike your corner of the world, however. Most of us live in communities where some can debate the choice between a Mercedes and a Volvo while others despair of coming up with the down payment for a fifteen-year old Chevy.

Wherever you live—mountains, prairie, desert, bayou—nature can stun you with its power, beauty and mystery. We live all of us in a delicate balance between the seen and the unseen, the everyday and the eternal. The best we can do is know our terrain, treasure the beauty along the way, and choose the vehicle that can best negotiate the snow and ice, the sand and mud, of our lives. What vehicle do you choose?

Waltzing With Bears

One of my favorite songs is *Waltzing With Bears*. For those who have never heard the lyrics, they tell the story of the singer's Uncle Walter and his penchant for waltzing with bears. No matter what the family does to discourage this practice, Walter manages to slip out in the middle of the night—and the wee small hours of the morning—and dance with bears. And his bears are diverse. Uncle Walter is no elitist: he dances with bears of all shapes, descriptions, genders, races and ethnicities. Bears, polar and panda. Uncle Walter's criteria is simple: You must be a bear and you must waltz.

Now, perhaps, you might say that, being an unashamed liberal, I love this song because Uncle Walter is such a true egalitarian. It's true that I rejoice in the vision of Uncle Walter twirling from bear to bear, bending with gentlemanly panache to waltz with the tiny koala and stretching arms—and courage—to grasp the grizzly's waist (if bears have waists). I see him bending and swirling with black bears, white bears, brown bears. I am happy that he doesn't cast off the raggy, the shaggy, the baggy.

Perhaps I feel that if such be his partners, I, too, would have a chance—were I a bear—to place my paw in Uncle Walter's hand and sway and spin to *The Blue Danube*. For often I feel raggy and shaggy and even baggy as life nips at my heels. And, though I can be snipped and combed and straightened, there are times when to be desired for the dance, even when a bit tatty at the edges, is a fantasy that lifts my heart. It is lovely to imagine that, even at my worst, I'd not be left out of Uncle Walter's waltzing.

Then again, there is the music itself, the waltzing rhythms of the song are those of a merry-go-round waltz, a gazebo dance hall at the fair ground, summer evenings in childhood when every day was delight, and the world was a happy family. All of that joy effervesces in the music, and all those memories of a time long lost when innocence was good and waltzing with bears seemed perfectly possible, for evil did not yet exist.

Yet, there is more even than the dream of childhood. For his relatives implore Uncle Walter to be respectable, to act more like them, to behave for goodness sake! And when he continues in his bear madness they fear he is forever lost.

Ah, there's the other side of childhood, the other side of adulthood. Don't we all sometimes get tired of being told to behave ourselves, to do our duty and brush our teeth with vigor? I confess I do. Sometimes I'd like to send in a note: *No Sermon This Week. Reverend Sarah is waltzing with bears.*

What I really love about Uncle Walter is not his exemplary egalitarianism nor even his courage to face the claws and fangs (for we are told his clothes are much the worse from dancing with bears). No, what I love about Uncle Walter is his subversion! He's not going to bed at night. He's sneaking out to waltz! I love his totally irresponsible approach to life as his family knows it and his refusal to give up his passion.

Oh, he is not heartless. When his family begs him to stay, (I can almost hear them pleading with him, "Uncle Walter, life is real; life is earnest!") Uncle Walter, his eyes twinkling and his feet tapping, succumbs just enough to give the family one day. But, then, what joy, the lyrics proclaim that the bears reclaimed Uncle Walter and even now, as you read this, somewhere in the sunlit forest or the starlit glade, Uncle Walter is waltzing with bears.

What rapture to be so good at your chosen vocation that your public will not allow your family to imprison you in their conventional wisdom. Of course, for most of us, the conventional wisdom works, but for those few among us who can waltz with bears, may the rest of us have the wisdom and joy to send them waltzing with our blessing!

Note: In doing research I discovered that this song's original title was "Uncle Terwilliger Waltzes with Bears" and the words are by non-other than the beloved and delightful Dr. Seuss, which explains a lot! The music is by Eugene Poddany. The song was first printed in *The Cat in the Hat Songbook,* published by Random House, Inc. in 1967. *Waltzing with Bears* is a favorite of many singers, folk and otherwise. Robbie Clemment sings it on the recording "Magic Place" and Gordon Bok, Anne Muir, and Ed Trickett on "Minneapolis Concert". There are probably other recordings as well. Buy one, play it. I guarantee it will lift your spirits and set your feet a-dancing.

For the Eeyore in All of Us

As I sit here on a hot August day, fall seems light years away. I am not one of those people who on the Fourth of July announce mournfully, "Summer is almost over."

"Actually, summer isn't over until the Autumn Equinox in late September," I blithely correct those sad souls who insist on reducing summer to a two week duration, one of which they complain is too hot, and the other, too rainy.

I realize my words are scoffed at as the blitherings of a Pollyanna. The folks who insist upon looking on the gloomy side will do so, no matter what. In fact, if they couldn't be unhappy, they'd be utterly miserable. I am not talking here about people who are sad because of life's tribulations, the clinically depressed, or those just having a bad day. I am talking about the Eeyores of the world, who like the kindly, sad donkey in *Winnie the Pooh*, really do not feel secure unless they are insecure, who cannot be happy without keeping a firm hold on their misery. I know these people well because I have had my turn at being one, and probably will again. Fortunately, for most of us, our Eeyore moods are usually quickly lifted by a reminder that indeed summer is not over in two weeks, the cup is half full with a suitably delectable ambrosia, and rainy days can be fun if you make fudge with a friend, sit by a quiet fire, or just listen to the rain melodying on your roof. Life is indeed sweet.

But as Eeyore, or more correctly, Hamlet, would say, "There's the rub." The sweetness of life only makes life sadder. Why shouldn't we all be melancholics, as the Renaissance dubbed their Eeyores; for the stark truth is we are aware of the sweet melancholy of life. We know too well that all joy is fleeting, that disease and disaster loom, death comes at the end, and the deeper our loves, the deeper our losses.

We humans face a choice between the bitter melancholy of a life spent bemoaning the unfairness of it all and walling ourselves off from love and friendship to avoid the pain, or the sweet melancholy of a life spent rejoicing at whatever splendors life bestows upon us, agonizing at the sorrows that rend our hearts, giving and receiving love and comfort to friends, family, and fellow comrades on the journey, living fully.

Sweet melancholy acknowledges that both sides of our nature, the sadness and the gladness, are necessary. If we gloried in the beauty of the rain and did not cry out at the destruction of the flood, we would be heartless. If we weep at death and devastation and do not delight in birth and creation, we will succumb to despair. If we open our hearts with love to life and death, we will live fully—with pain and joy, tears and laughter, anger and gentleness, confusion and clarity—the whole human mix of terrible sweetness. And sometimes amidst our pain and joy we will feel the mystery informing our melancholy and our joy, the mystery stirring us to hope beyond sadness, beyond pain, beyond terror; hope that as we live joyfully through love, love will sustain us even unto and beyond death.

What I Learned on My Summer Vacation

This summer I went on a trip in Maine with an old friend of mine, who lives in Maine. We've done this often, and we've developed a pattern. We like to revisit places we love and we like to visit one place we've never been. Maine is a big state, we would need another lifetime to see everything!

This year our new place was Monhegan Island, an art and lobstering village ten miles off the coast. We stayed on the mainland at Port Clyde and took the ferry out for the day. We managed to get lost on the way to Port Clyde. However, we don't really consider ourselves lost when we get off track, we just say, "Hey, some scenery we didn't expect to see, great!" In this case we then turned around, ignored the map and followed my friend's instinct, straight to Moody's Diner in Waldeboro for lunch. This is not a meditation about the joys of Moody's Diner, except to say, that if you ever get lost or found near Waldeboro, revive your body and spirit at Moody's.

This meditation isn't even about Monhegan, although I do advise the island as a place to restore your soul to peace. You truly feel in a different, and friendlier, world out there. Although perhaps it is about Monhegan's saving grace, for it was at the Scruffy Dog on the island that my friend and I resolved a conflict that although it hadn't exactly threatened our friendship, had ruffled the waters.

What causes conflicts between friends? World issues of great note? Sometimes, perhaps. But more often it is something completely inconsequential. In our case, it was a jacket. It had gotten a bit chilly in Port Clyde, and as I was going to the car, my friend asked me to bring back her gray jacket. Sounds easy, right? Except that I couldn't find a gray jacket. I looked in the hatch, in the back, in the front, no gray jacket. There was, however, a brown jacket. That surely would suffice.

"Sorry, can't find your gray jacket but here's your brown one," I said.

"Brown! This jacket is gray." My friend replied, with a note of incredulity, that I could call her jacket brown.

"No, it's brown."

"It's gray, Sarah, I wish it were brown. I like brown much better, but this is definitely gray."

"You got to be kidding. It's brown"

"Brown.—Gray.—Brown.—Gray."

"Maybe a grayish brown," I conceded

"There's no brown in this at all." My friend was emphatic.

"Okay," I replied. We've been friends a long time. I didn't want us to founder on the shoals of color discrimination.

"I wish it were brown," my friend replied, making peace by suggesting that she agreed that brown was a superior color.

We turned to enjoying the sunset, the smell of the sea, the call of the gulls.

But I secretly brooded. I was worried. I knew my friend was completely convinced that her jacket was gray. She was not playing games with my mind. Just as I was convinced her jacket was brown, with maybe a twinge of gray. Taking that as true, it appeared that one of us was wrong, which could mean I had some kind of esoteric color blindness. I had never heard of brown-gray female color blindness, but new dysfunctions are discovered every day. If only I could get my friend to say there was just a hint of brown in her jacket. But I realized that any more discussion could lead to disaster. I banished the jacket from my conscious mind, but subconsciously a little voice kept saying," It's brown!" or "Make a doctor's appointment as soon as you get back."

The next morning we took the ferry to Monhegan, both in agreement that the fog was gray, and the sun was breaking through. We rambled along the dirt roads on the island and hungry, we sat down on the open air porch of the Scruffy Dog to savor our sea food and the sea air. I stood up to open the door to the restaurant for a woman with a cane. As I did so, I was filled with courage, for she had on a coat that to me was the perfect gray. If I was wrong, it meant the eye doctor. If I was right . . . .

"Look," I said to my friend, "This lady's jacket is gray." As the elder gave me a questioning glance, I explained, "My friend and I have been arguing. I say her jacket is brown, and she says it's gray. Now yours I say is gray. What would you call hers?"

My friend held up her jacket. I held my breath.

The infinitely wise woman said, "Brown. No doubt about it."

"Thank you, thank you," I cried. "It's been driving me crazy."

"No, it's not," protested my friend. "I love brown, but this is gray."

Now the Scruffy Dog is not a formal restaurant. It's the kind of place where people feel free to contribute to any conversation they can overhear. A middle-age woman with an authoritative air, strode over, took the jacket in hand, and confronted my friend. "This jacket is definitely brown. You have to be crazy to think it is gray."

"Not so," yelled her husband from their table, "It's gray."

"Putty"

"Taupe"

"Pewter"

Monhegan does have a lot of artists, remember.

"Brown, brown, brown"

Everyone cast a vote.

"All right, Sarah, I still consider my jacket gray, but I can see there is a—

"Three out of four say brown," I exulted.

"A chance it may have some little bit of brown in it." My friend has no anxieties about color blindness.

The sun shone. We all had a good laugh. I mentally cancelled the eye appointment.

The next day in a shop in Blue Hill, Maine, I picked up a magnet with a photo of two dachshunds, back to back. Once you become the person of a dachshund, you become a convert to dachshund memorabilia. But this was more than just cute dachsies, for underneath the two opposite dogs were the words: "A friendship with two viewpoints is twice as strong."

I showed it to my friend, and we both chuckled. Ah, yes. Us to the tee.

Learning that two friends can have distinctly different viewpoints may not sound like a big news flash to you. But it is one that we need to remind ourselves of often. Two friends can have different views—both can be right or wrong—what's more it can strengthen a friendship. Although sometimes it may take help from unbiased bystanders to remind them that not only are there are two viewpoints, they are often five or six or more, remember, taupe, putty, pewter.

In our personal lives with friends, family, co-workers, it is good to remind ourselves of those dachshunds—and respect our differences of opinion—even rejoice in the ways they strengthen our friendships. In the sampling at the Scruffy Dog, brown did win out over gray, but as I kept looking at the jacket, I started to appreciate that gray tones were there. I started to realize that my friend could see something it took me a long time to perceive.

So, it is in healthy groups and healthy personal relationships, when we stop to listen, to respect, and to love, our minds and hearts open. People share, listen, grow. People discover that by opening up, instead of closing down, by allowing for different viewpoints, we create relationships that are constantly perceiving new colors in our life together. What will be the next color in your rainbow with the people in your life? Fuchsia, crimson, strawberry? Find out—together!

The Path Most Taken

"To learn something new, take the path you took yesterday."
                                                     John Burroughs

There is great excitement in first impressions. A few weeks ago I saw a pelican for the first time. I laughed and clapped my hands. What a glory is a pelican! How did the creator ever come up with such a useful and humorous design?

Yet I have seen sea gulls since childhood, and never cease to be amazed at the glory of the sea gull. The soaring, gliding, cacophonous seagull! Another design award for the creator! Now after all these years, I see not only sea gulls, but each sea gull and not only each sea gull, but this particular sea gull on this particular day showing me something new about what it is to be a sea gull. The sea gull strut and sway, when earthbound they turn into Charlie Chaplin-like walkers. The sea gull snap and flurry as sea gull obstreperous pushes away sea gull meek and mild. Sea gulls with broken wings, sea gulls nesting, sea gulls dive bombing as humans wave sticks to protect their hapless human heads from the depredations of claw, beak and worse. Each sea gull teaches me anew of seagullness.

Were I to have the chance to see a pelican a second time what news would I learn from pelican world? Perhaps see a pelican lunching with that great trencher of a bill? Stare eye to beady eye. Hear the pelican voicing complaints or delights? Once is not enough—to know a path, we must traverse it often, learning anew each time.

In a world in which novelty and new experiences rank high, it is good to consider John Burroughs' words—to retain a few paths we walk frequently learning something new each time. Our spiritual paths are such paths, whether we walk the path of prayer, meditation, reading, church worship, song. We need to keep returning to our spiritual paths to revitalize ourselves. We learn something new each time from the twists and turns, the sudden sunlight and

18

rain, the branches that slap our faces and the stalwart reliable limbs we can grab on to when we stumble. Spiritual paths reveal new insights each time we walk them. The more often we put our feet on the path, the more we are strengthened and renewed. What have you learned today on your spiritual path?

Taffy Comes Into His Own

I was having trouble sleeping. Two-thirty a.m., the red numerals blinked at me. The dog curled up in peaceful slumber at the foot of the bed. A faithful companion most of the time, but at 2:30 a.m., blissfully asleep. The cat, however, was awake. He prowled around the dog. Unable to evoke a response, he let the sleeping dog lie. He saw me, sitting up bleary-eyed, trying to decide which insomnia remedy to try: milk, reading, a video? The cat purred. Joy, he seemed to say, at last company in the middle of the night. The human is on my schedule finally. He strolled up to my pillow, the motor really humming now. I patted his head. He squinted up his eyes in pleasure. At last the human is behaving as a cat. He sprinted lithely onto my chest and raised his head as if to ask: How far has the human advanced? I scratched under his chin. The cat preened. Dare I suggest the cat smiled? The purr reverberated like a miniature outboard motor. The cat snuggled on the quilt, a pleasant heaviness. See, he seemed to challenge me, I too can be affectionate when I wish—when you stop trying to make me into the Other.

His golden fur shone. His yellow eyes gleamed. His name is Taffy. He is a menace sometimes, catapulting himself to the counter top then to the refrigerator top and thence to the very top shelf beneath the ceiling, sending the baskets stored on the fridge cascading to the floor. Left to his own devices, he would sharpen his claws on the caning of the rocker. He fancies my jewelry, not to bedeck himself, but to push from the bureau to the floor and thence to play with instead of the toy mice, I so benevolently provide. I have had to rearrange my furniture and my life to accommodate his being. And for all my efforts, I have received polite indifference from him until tonight at 2:30 a.m.

As he purrs on, something happens in my heart, I let go of Dusty. For there was another cat in my life, a cat who at age seventeen staggered and dragged himself along for a week, until finally I admitted the time had come. I stood by his side, patting him tenderly, as the vet gently eased him into death. I will never have another cat, I proclaimed. No cat could be Dusty. But I do love cats.

Their grace, their independence, their sheer beauty, their mystery, all that is standard equipment with a cat, but not necessarily love, and Dusty had been a loving cat. Even more astonishing, he was a cat who wanted love. He'd jump in my lap; he'd curl up under my arm in bed. If sadness made me distant, Dusty was not to be deterred. He'd nuzzle my face or brush against me, as if to say, I'm here, I love you, life can't be so bad. And it wasn't.

I knew Taffy wasn't Dusty, but I did want him to be. Taffy has no patience for laps. He dashes and darts through the house, an entertaining presence. Sympathy does not interest him. I pick him up and cuddle him anyway, telling him, he needs to be loved, whether he knows it or not. (This according to the cat books is not the way you should treat a cat, instead you should honor his independence. Years ago when my children were little, I read a book that said you shouldn't cuddle children. I ignored that one, thankfully, and so now I ignore the cat expert.) Taffy has shrugged off my affection, wriggling free and galloping away, until our 2:30 a.m. meeting, when suddenly he settles in for a long purr and is pleased to be stroked and patted and admired. You see, he seems to say, I am not Dusty. I am Taffy. Learn to love me.

So it is with life, we hold onto the old or we try to turn the new into the old, when what we should do is remember the past with pleasure and love the present for its own blessings. Soon enough it too will be a memory. Hold the present to your heart. Love each creature and each place for its own specialness. And may you be blessed with a loving cat.

Prune Away Your Guilt and Plant

Your Bliss

I want to be in the church garden patch. I have a great garden guilt—the patch looks much more like a patch right now than a garden. I can almost hear people looking over the railing and muttering angrily, "Who has let this garden go to wrack and ruin. Have they no shame!" Grass is overgrown. Dandelions rule. The pansies are surviving, but it is in spite of not being watered. How long can they last without my tender, loving care? There is a delightful surprise an absolutely thriving violet I don't remember planting. However, my plant congregation is in need of my ministry. My fingers are itching to wield the trowel, to cruise the nurseries for new flowers, to stand up with a well-earned backache and see a garden in bloom.

My guilt is assuaged only by the chill in the air. Perhaps this is not the most auspicious day for transplanting from nursery to earth. And of course there is my other guilt—all the inside work I have to get done before I can hit the garden. Just do it, I urge myself, and then when the sun warms my back, as it will any day now, I can dig to my heart's content. Meanwhile I have plenty of inside chores including a lot of pruning in my office in which paper grows like weeds. I discover that the imperative call of the garden concentrates my mind. If I buckle down and do all my to-do list on this gray day, I will be free, free, free when the temperature hits seventy again. I perk up. I tap on the keyboard. I look at my office with the eyes of someone about to conquer Mt. Everest. I can do it! If I were more talented musically, I'd start whistling while I work. What had seemed like terrible chores to trudge through, now are becoming energizing hurdles to leap over on my way to my destination—marigolds, lupines, roses, zinnias, here I come!

And how nice it will be after a few hours in the good earth, to come into a spruced-up office, and finally do what I always thought ministers did so much of—read theology, have a friendly chat with a parishioner, silently meditate over a cup of green tea on the mystery of the universe. Ah, yes, bliss awaits. What guilt is bothering you? What is keeping you from your bliss? Take my advice: prune away your guilt and plant your bliss!

Alex—A Conversation

"Hi," the little voice chirped into the phone. I am thrilled. Alex is saying "Hi" to me. Loud and clear.

His parents have been worried because Alex will be two the end of August and is not yet much of a talker. I have not been so worried. He seems too busy running around looking at everything, industriously putting things away (a talent which neither my sons nor I have yet mastered) and tracing the letters on every sign he comes across. It seems to me Alex is giving precedence to his tactile and motor skills. He toddles with such joy! As if to say, "Hey, what an amazing thrill this is! I can move under my own power. Whoopee!" We grown-ups forget what a wonderful discovery walking must be.

Even more reassuring for me is the fact that the first word Alex did say clearly and repeatedly was a word that impressed me mightily since it wasn't one I usually associate with first utterances. That word is "Outside" accompanied by a tugging on the doorknob, just in case his parents and grandparents are too benighted to get his drift. What this says to me is that here is a child who knows how to talk when he has something he wants to say, but sees no reason to sit around shooting the breeze, yakking aimlessly.

His parents not feeling quite so reassured got Alex and themselves some expert help. Whether nature or the therapist worked the magic, Alex is now saying "Hi" and "Bye" to everyone, and in fact has learned some new words his parents are not too happy about, including the one every parent learns to rue, "NO".

What my son and daughter-in-law are learning is that worry and children go together.

What I am learning is that grandchildren bedazzle the grandparent no matter what.

What Alex is learning is that there are a goodly number of big people in his life for whom he is the center of their love.

If only this were true for all children, what might happen in this world?

Meanwhile I await eagerly, the next word from Alex.

Fireplace Dreams

I miss a fireplace. A working fireplace. Or rather, a fireplace of delights and dreams—and real logs, real fire. I grew up with a fireplace in our living room, not used for heat, but for warmth, beauty, visions, friendliness. We carefully cleaned the fireplace each Christmas Eve, so Santa would not be covered in ash. On Christmas Day, we lit the fire using as kindling the few Christmas wrappings my mother deemed unsalvageable for another year. The fireplace crackled, snapped, and exuded good cheer all December 25th and New Year's as it did on Thanksgiving, and on snowy January, February, and March days and evenings.

The fire removed the chill of fog in fall and spring, and in the hurricane became briefly a working fireplace, for heat, for light, for cooking, most of all, for the vision of coziness amidst the tempest's roar. Even in summer, when the days turned damp and shivery, the fire would be lit and we'd gather in its glow for fun and games. I still have the old wire popcorn popper we jiggled above the flames, waiting with bated breath for that first distinctive POP and then in exultation as the kernels exploded in a delicious cacophony of pows! I have lost, years ago, the wire marshmallow and hot dog toasters that the bold thrust into the flames (those of us who liked blackened marshmallows and hot dogs that split, taking the risk of losing them to the fire god) and the more genteel held with tense concentration hovering over the embers for perfectly browned outside, sumptuously melted inside, marshmallows.

I remember my thirteenth birthday an icy, wind-whistling, February night when ten teen girls toasted and roasted and tried to scare each other silly with ghost stories as the fire died slowly down and the room grew dark—until mother returned with hot chocolate and in her matter of fact manner stirred up the fire with a poker, adding a new log for good measure, breaking the spell of titillating terror. We turned to giggling over riddles, jokes, and songs featuring a lot of mindless alliteration.

I remember the dinner parties as an adult when talk would turn from children to gossip to politics to God—somehow the fire drew us into an intimacy and warmth that went beyond the heat upon our faces. I remember so many faces, some grown, some gone, but all faces that turned more friendly around the fire, that gentled into peace, sharing the best of themselves in the steadfast glow.

If you have such a fireplace, invite your friends over, stockpile wood for the storm, or light a log alone and listen to the fire's song. If, like me, your fireplace is in a room long gone from you, remember those of your past and those who shared them, and be thankful. Remember also those who have sat with you beside all the fires of your life, those who need no fireplace of bricks and mortar to laugh with you, and eat with you, and share your fears and delights. The fireplace may no longer be in my life, but the fires of friendship are—and so may it be with you.

Lap-Time

I sit with a warm puppy on my lap. I should have left her home, but it would have meant eight hours of crate time for the day, and that seemed just too much! So to work with me came Nelly, the mini-dachshund puppy with a nose for everything and stubs of legs with the power of propellers. Which is to say she is fast and furious, fearless and endlessly curious. Contemplation is not her basic mode. Social action is Nelly's game.

Nelly lost no time in finding devious ways to occupy herself. She succeeded in quietly gnawing a cover off a 19th century book (mine, not the church's). I was more worried about the effect of over a hundred years of book mites (or whatever little creatures make their home in old books), then on the loss of the cover, but as her intent seemed more to rip than ingest, that fear was unfounded. She then upped the ante by stealing the tennis ball of the more sedate elder dog, Sadie, companion to our administrator, Linda. Sadie was unruffled, even aloof, choosing not to engage with the young scamp. Rebuffed, Nelly proceeded to turn over a flower pot complete with dirt, which she examined for edible remnants, backing away only as I blasted the vacuum cleaner in her direction. All this occurred as I was tapping my way through my overflowing e-mail account, responding and deleting with as much zeal as Nelly applied to tugging down and eating scraps of unfiled papers. So if I can't find that report you sent me, when I say the dog ate it, you must take me at my word.

Finally, I took notice before even more egregious acts of doggy daring could be perpetrated, and walked young Nell around the perimeters of our fine establishment. She examined underneath all the bushes with the zeal of the hound she is, seeming to find great delight in the scents of detritus and holly alike. Upon return, Nelly was calm for about thirty seconds and then pranced up to me and deposited a well-gnawed, cardboard tube embellished with the words, TAKE A TUBE. Interpreting these words literally, I picked up the tube-shaped dog, plunked her on my lap, and continued with my work in peace. It seemed that all Nelly really wanted was to be held.

As she settled into her perch, I recalled all the other critters who raised cain in my life, until I stopped and held them. My children who, as Nelly, actually wanted lap time, but also the others who wanted to be held in my attention, the students who wanted me to listen to them; the old lady who called me up and said, it's time you visited me; the friends who in their pain needed me to hold their hand, take them in my arms, or simply reassure them across the telephone wires, "I love you." Sometimes all any of us want and need is to be held—sometimes all any of us can do for our loved ones is hold them. And so often that is enough.

Valentine's Day for Everyone

When I was a child, Valentine's Day was one of the highlights of our school year. Halfway between the serious observances in honor of Lincoln and Washington, there suddenly appeared in our classroom a magical-looking box festooned with lace doilies and red hearts and fairly breathing expectation. Into that box we dropped our valentines, purchased at the dime store in packages of forty (thirty-nine small ones for classmates and one slightly larger for the teacher). Classes were bigger in those days, even in my small town, about thirty-five to a room, and the rule was strict that you had to give Valentines to everyone. Miss Jolikko, Mrs. Hale, and Mrs. Paradis did not want to deal with tears from any quarter—equality was to reign. Although they couldn't stop some particularly popular little girls getting more than one Valentine from a smitten young swain, they could enforce the law that no one went without the regulation thirty-five.

Buying the Valentines and deciding who was to get which one was as much fun as getting them. The bright red, white and gold displays, the funny pictures, the silly rhymes burst into the mud-bespattered, gray slush days of winter at its dreariest and pronounced, "See, winter can be fun. It's time to celebrate Love and Friendship and Jokes and Beauty!"

Valentine's Day was not a religious holiday to us. Even historically Valentine's Day as a holiday of romance has little or no relationship to St. Valentine. The custom of giving cards to sweethearts developed in medieval Europe because it was believed that mid-February was the time when birds began to mate. Bird biology, whether accurate or not, translated into the idea that mid-February was a time to celebrate human lovebirds.

As I grew up, and in the words of St. Paul "put away childish things," I stopped sending Valentines. I subscribed to the belief that Valentine's Day was for lovers only. Valentine's Day became a non-event, a day accenting my lack of a partner, or at best a day to recall happy memories. As I started to think of those memories, I realized that my happiest Valentine's Days had nothing to do with sweethearts, but with friends and family. There were my childhood Valentine mornings when I'd find a small gift beside my breakfast plate, the school Valentine parties, the afternoons of paste and glory when my sons and I made Valentines, the Valentine gifts to my children and cards to friends—lovely cheerful missives arriving to brighten a wintry day.

And so I propose to you, that Valentine's Day is for all of us, partnered or simply friended. Valentine's Day is an opportunity to send an outrageously romantic or funny card to a friend—a card that reminds you both of the joy of friendship. No, I'm not a stockholder in a card company, but I do think there is something very special about finding among the bills and advertising flyers a genuinely delightful card full of whimsy and whim. I recommend to you that you trot yourself over to either the card store or the arts and crafts emporium for a supply of lacy doilies, paste and red construction paper. Make or buy some cards to send to friends. Spread a little joy this February—tell your friends just how happy you are to have them in your life! As you slip the cards into the mailbox, you'll feel a frisson of delight—the delight that comes from sending a friend a magical, mystical Valentine—the delight that comes from being a Valentine. And now, if you'll excuse me, I have some Valentine card shopping to do!

Mother's Day—My Mother & The Wind

I love wind. The more blustery the better. Great gusts, lashing waves, torrential downpours. That's my kind of weather! I love being safe in my house, nestled under comforters, dog snuggled up beside me, cat purring at my feet, windows rattling, raindrops splashing on the panes, a good book, and crisp apples. Heaven on earth! I love being out in the wind, gusts blowing through me, waking me up to the power and glory of air. Again, Heaven on earth!

I have a friend who hates wind. She had some bad experiences in childhood with Brother Wind. But she tells me that since making my acquaintance, the wind bothers her less. Instead of worrying about the roof being ripped off her house, she thinks, "Ah, Sarah, must be happy!"

It goes to show how we can infect others with our enthusiasms. I myself was so infected with wind enthusiasm by my mother. Yes, I confess, as a child I cowered when the wind blew. I worried that the trees might fall on the house or the telephone wires, and then Va-Voom—curtains for the Clark family.

My mother had no such trepidations. One fierce Northeaster my father had gone into Boston with the Gloucester High Football team to appear on a TV show, in his role as sports reporter. We had no TV but a friend who lived on Front Beach did. My mother was not about to let a Northeaster (we called them Northeasters, not Nor'easters), interfere with her seeing her husband's TV debut. Seeing me head for the closet, my mother shoved my coat in my arms, and said, "Nothing to be afraid of. This is only a Northeaster, not a hurricane."

She explained that a full-scale hurricane would have caused Front Beach to flood into the cemetery, covering the sidewalk and road, and in that case, the better part of valor might have been to stay indoors. But a Northeaster, why, that was just wind, a few waves, "Look," she pointed out as we reached Front Beach, "Sidewalk's still here."

Then she turned to face the ocean. "Just feel that wind," she exulted. I turned. The wind gusted over and through me. A true elemental force. I felt swept clean of all the cobwebs and dust of life. The salty mix of rain and ocean sprayed my face, a Mother Nature baptism. I fell in love with the wind and the rain.

My mother tugged at my sleeve. On we went to the warmth and coziness of our friend's seaside home. A sprightly fire crackled, the TV crackled too, but we were still able to see my Dad. The wind whistled and rattled, the rain knocked and drummed; we had tea and cookies and gabbed about this momentous occasion and felt the wonderful safeness of friends sharing a haven in the storm.

Mom and I cheerfully battled our way home, once again stopping for a hardy spritz of Northeaster. Once back in our own snug harbor, we lit a fire to welcome Dad from his TV and storm adventures.

In this month of Mother's Day, I think of my mother who shoved timid me into so many adventures of life and thank her. Life is so much more exhilarating facing the wind than huddling in a closet.

What did your mother teach you? If she's still around, be sure to thank her! If she's no longer with you, take the time to remember her with love.

Father's Day—Free Love

Freedom is one of our most revered human values in the United States. June is the month we celebrate Flag Day, the major symbol of both American unity and American love of freedom. June is also the month we celebrate Father's Day, and freedom is not the major attribute of being a father. Becoming a parent requires us to give up much of our freedom. Not all of our freedom, certainly, but once we are parents, we must take into consideration the effect our actions will have on our children. We cannot take off to backpack through Europe, leaving our toddlers to make their way to day care on their own. Even a trip to the supermarket becomes a major expedition as we wrestle our young into snowsuits, load them into the car, and brave the aisles trying to get food and not lose a child in the process.

As fathers become more and more active in their children's lives, men are discovering how exhausting fatherhood is, and how much of their freedom has to be put on the shelf until that day when the youngster gets in the car and drives off to his or her first real job, first real apartment. Suddenly Dad's freedom almost returns—never completely because always, always fathers worry.

Sometime along the line, fathers realize that freedom no longer means freedom from children, but instead freedom to be with their children. Freedom to have the time to be good parents. Fathers discover the joys of loss of freedom, the joys of being bound to their children.

Some fathers never discover that joy, and fearful of the loss of personal freedom, sadly, opt out of fatherhood. Some take to the road, never to be heard of again. Others build up barricades of work and busyness, providing financially for their children, but being emotionally absent. Fortunately most fathers embrace their loss of freedom and find themselves feeling sorry for that lonely guy over there shopping without the aid of a five-year-old's advice on the best cereal to purchase.

Would a father really want to sleep late rather than be out in the brisk fall air watching his son or daughter play soccer? Who puts photos of sleeping late in their photo albums or CD-ROMs? But who forgets their children's birthday parties—the snowmen you made together—the camping trips—or just the simple walks around the block, kicking the leaves, talking, being together father and child in loving communion. At such times both father and children are truly free in each other's love.

For wonderful as freedom is even more wonderful is giving yourself freely to another human being. Fathers and mothers know that, in truth, they are the freest people in the world.

Mother's (and Father's) Day for All of Us

Mother's Day will be upon us in May with all its blessings and curses. I say this because it has become increasingly difficult to celebrate Mother's and Father's Day in churches. Some people don't like Mother's and Father's Day on the grounds that these celebrations were made up by merchants to get our money. Certainly shops and restaurants have taken full advantage of the opportunity to ring up sales—but what is so terrible about people taking a day out of the year to spend a little extra on Ma and Pa? Is it so hard to send your mother a card? I have the feeling that most of the people who complain are just being defensive because they forgot—or worse because their children forget! So just to make it easier for you absent-minded folk:. MARK THE DATES DOWN NOW. BETTER YET BUY YOUR CARDS AND PRESENTS NOW. AND MARK YOUR CALENDAR AS TO TIME OF DELIVERY. MAKE MOM AND DAD HAPPY. (If you have absent-minded children, send them this!)

Harder to deal with are all the people who claim Mother's and Father's Days makes them sad because they had a bad parent, or their parent is dead, or they are not parents, so they feel left out. We have become a nation, nay a world, of defenders of our rights—a world where if everyone isn't included in everything than we can't have the event. I usually approve of this stance, but sometimes even I think we go too far. It is a tragedy that someone had a bad mother or father, yet why should that translate into no one else ever having the right to praise good mothers and fathers? Shouldn't it be the opposite, that we should hold up the ideal of what it is to be a good parent rather than stifling all references to good mothers and fathers?

Yes, Mother's and Father's Day are sad for those of us whose good parents have died, but it is a sweet sadness, a day to take the time to remember, to let the gates of memory open. Surely our mothers and fathers would not want us to blot them out of our minds and hearts. Not that it takes Mother's or Father's Day to make me remember my parents, the memories of people we have truly loved are woven into our daily lives, helping us face the trials of life, and take pleasure at the victories. "Your mother and father would be proud!" people say, and we smile, for yes, it is good to bring Mom and Dad again into the circle of the present, smiling proudly at us, part of our achievement.

For those who are not biological mothers or fathers, you are not left out if you have ever along the road of life been a mother or father to another person in the best sense of those words—offered comfort, guidance, love, given of yourself to help another. If you have, then you can claim parenthood too, and bask in the glory of having been a good parent. If you haven't, then get to it! This year make an effort to be, if only for a few moments, a good parent to some creature in need of comfort, be they human or animal. The world needs us to be good mothers and fathers to all of creation. To remind us of our parental responsibilities, we need Mother's and Father's Day! So let's all celebrate—then, no one need be left out.

Good and Evil—On The News Today

Pillars of the community dissolve before our eyes. A mayor arrested for pedophilia. A woman convicted of a brutal murder committed twenty-three years ago. The tip of the iceberg of their lives was sweetness and light, good neighbors, happy families, members of religious communities, hard workers. The iceberg hidden by the waters was darkness and evil . . . no other word, but evil.

We feel a punch in the gut, a stab in the heart, a quiver of fear when the news breaks. How could this be? We ate lunch together, talked about toilet training and teaching teens to drive, sang hymns of love, worked building a house as a justice project. They were so pleasant, so good, even their spouses were unaware of their other side. It must be a mistake.

They confess. They bargain for lighter sentences. They express regret with their lips. We sense the regret is at being caught, not for their actions. How can people be split in two like this? The good and the bad in one mind and body. Nothing in our religion prepares us.

Perhaps for Christians, Judas is a reminder. But somehow Judas doesn't help us understand the woman who leads the Girl Scout troop and kills her loving husband because she lusted for another man. Divorce was unacceptable in her church, she pleaded. Murder was acceptable? No, murder undetected was a boon to her—a new husband and children in an upscale suburb, until twenty years later the detectives knocked on her door.

We ask ourselves how they live with themselves, these people who one day decorate the parish hall for a children's party and that evening in another part of town rape a ten-year-old? What goes through their minds as later they slip into bed next to their wife? Could it be uncontrollable, some errant gene, mental illness? Yet for most of their lives, they did control themselves. We ask ourselves—are we capable of such evil?

The iceberg looms—high in the sun goodness, beneath in the dark cold waters, evil. The need to be on guard constantly against the evil without and within reinforces itself. The need to discern good from evil, to choose good over evil. Still we cry out why? Why is there evil? No answer except the reminder that as there is evil, there is good. To survive, we must remember the good and choose the good.

Then There is Grace

A wedding an hour before sunset on a hot day, the cloud-cover cooling the grove, the rain waiting for another day. A garden beside a quiet, tree-shaded pond. Chairs on the grass, everyone close enough to be truly part of the ceremony, the sweetness of the wedding party, the two families, the children, the friends at this moment all in accord to give the young couple a sacred blessing. A well-planned time of grace, yet grace is never automatic. No amount of planning can create grace amongst disharmony of spirits, and grace can emerge in the chaos of ceremonies where all goes outwardly awry. For grace is nothing more than the sudden heart-stirring realization, that, however briefly, we are all held together by absolute love.

The grand moments announce that grace like a bugle call, but grace reaches out to us in the quiet moments as well. This morning I woke early and sat in peace in my room nested amongst the trees, the greenery stirring my soul. Alone, yet not alone, held by absolute love.

Grace is always here. It is we who are more often not.

Stop and allow yourself to be aware of the grace in your life.

Be held by absolute love.

Use It or Lose It

In the drama class I taught, I had two rules: "Use it" and "Leave your baggage at the door." Sound opposite, don't they? "Use it" means if you are having a problem, i.e., a cold, a broken love affair, a fight with your mother, use those emotions to enhance your acting. Instead of fighting the cough, the depression, the anger, see how you can use it to add nuance to the character you are playing. Sometimes it works and the actor discovers a new dimension to the role; the problem becomes part of the solution. Sometimes it doesn't work and then you turn to "Leave your baggage at the door"—wipe out the heartbreak for the duration and concentrate on being the comic, the invincible one, whatever your character is.

Leaving your baggage also applied to any misgivings you might have about your fellow actors. Teaching high school there were often different cliques in a classroom, but my rule was that baggage had to be left at the door—here we were together in mutual respect. Not always easy to achieve but usually by opening night, the play had created an ensemble in which the only clique was the troupe.

Recently when I got some bad cholesterol counts, I remembered those rules. First of all: Use it. I purchased some low fat, low cholesterol cookbooks. I now have a whole new relationship with lentils. I've discovered that all the burners on my stove work. I like the excitement of trying out new recipes. I've returned to walking long jaunts instead of just the short circuit from workplace to couch. The dog is particularly enjoying working his magic on ever new and more faraway shrubs.

I also was distressed at the bad news. I am a vegetarian. I thought I was already on a health diet. How could this be happening? Should I be afraid? That's where leave the baggage at the door comes in. Fear is helpful to jumpstart you into action—in this case, the diet and exercise. After that, fear is baggage best left at the door. So the suitcase marked fear, trembling, panic is on the deck with stickers on it: Destination—Down the River.

How about you? What baggage do you need to use? What should you leave at the door?

Give Yourself Soul Time—

A December Gift

Advent in the Christian tradition is a time of waiting expectantly for the light of God to return to a world darkened by human despair and cruelty. To signify their faith that the light will triumph over darkness, Christians light Advent candles of love, hope, peace, and joy lighting the way to the birth of Jesus. Christmas, a time to rejoice in being Christian, dedicated to a way of love and peace.

Hanukkah in the Jewish tradition is a time of waiting expectantly for new oil to be prepared to light the menorah. Recalling a miracle of light, candles burning eight nights from one cruse of oil. To signify their faith that light will triumph over darkness, Jews light the Hanukkah candles for eight nights, rejoicing in God's gift of liberty and light. Hanukkah, a time to rejoice in being Jewish, dedicated to a way of love and justice.

Solstice in the neo-pagan tradition is a time of waiting expectantly for the earth to turn from deepest darkness and cold to dawning light and warmth. To signify their faith that light will triumph over darkness, neo-pagans light candles as the ancient pagans lit bonfires to welcome the return of the sun, rejoicing in the beneficence of the universe. Solstice, a time to rejoice in being neo-pagan, dedicated to a way of love and beauty.

Yet the world is beset by war, injustice, and the degradation of nature's beauty. Still we are waiting. Advent is a time of intentional waiting in the darkness. This waiting is experienced as a grace, not an annoyance. Advent is a time to be still in the darkness, to see the good in the darkness as well as in the light. In the contemplative waiting of Advent, we open ourselves to the essence, the flame that lights our soul.

Rather than overwhelming yourself with frantic material preparations for your holy days and holidays, give yourself some Advent time for soul preparation.

You do not have to be Christian to need some Advent time—the holidays assault all of us—so take a lesson from Christianity, and give yourself some Advent peace.

Light a candle in the darkness and sit in the quiet. Read poetry in the early morning light before the workday. Play music that calms your spirit. Walk the woods, the beach, the winter garden. Visit the sunrise or sunset in solitude. Sit in silence with a friend. Lift your face to the snowflakes. Prepare yourself for the time of jubilant celebration with a time of serene contemplation. Face the darkness with the strength and peace that comes from holy stillness. Wait expectantly, with hope, faith, love, and your holy days will find you ready to receive the joy of the season.

Give yourself Advent by whatever name you wish to call it: my choice is Soul-Time!

Jesus at Christmas

Jesus born in a manger, lowly and poor. Jesus, the newborn king, with angelic host proclaiming. Jesus bursting on the scene in marvelous ambiguity. Who is he, king or peasant? Victor or victim? Protector of the status quo or revolutionary overturning the old order? Jesus, meek and mild, blessing the little children or Jesus, ferocious and furious, whipping the merchants out of the temple. The baby Jesus, smiling up at the magi with their glittering gifts, lifted up from the manger to be cradled in his mother's arms. The man Jesus, crowned with thorns, pierced through by spear, lowered down from the cross to be cradled one last time in his mother's arms.

The baby Jesus is the image most beloved. Babies, kittens, puppies, who doesn't love the young of whatever species? The baby Jesus threatens no one. We can all agree about the baby in the hay. Sweet, cute, innocent, good, the baby Jesus reminds us to love all children. The baby Jesus brings out the best in us. We open our hearts and our wallets as the carolers sing, "What Child is This?"

The man Jesus, that is where the ambivalence begins. What man is this? The question resounds in the Gospels: Son of God? Son of Man? King of the Jews? Messiah? Carpenter's son? Rabbi? Heretic? Terrorist? Healer? Savior? The question propels the scholars. Each generation of academics produces a new edition of Jesus. Each person creates a personal vision of Jesus.

The answer to the question some Christians paste on their car bumpers, "What would Jesus do?" depends largely on who is your Jesus. Many liberals would scoff at the question thinking it reveals a simplistic mind. Yet the question has merit to me, for it makes me ask again, who is Jesus? What does he require of me?

In the Episcopal church in which I grew up, there is a painting titled "Christ Comes to Rockport". He is standing on T-Wharf, surrounded by lobstermen and sundry villagers. As I remember it, Jesus looks quite at home, but the people appear somewhat stunned. The picture asks us, "What would we do if Jesus were here among us?" Would we respond to his teachings of love thy God, love each other, give up your wealth and serve the poor? Or would we listen and nod and then go back to life as usual. Throw the lobster pots in the boat and sail out of the harbor. Or mention to the police that perhaps this lad should be watched, he is a bit of a crank, possibly even a socialist, or worse, a union organizer. Would we follow Jesus or nail him back up on the cross?

We can love the baby Jesus who asks nothing of us except to love the sweetness of infancy. Can we love Jesus the man who makes demands? The Jesus who asks us the most critical question of all: not what would Jesus do, but what are you doing?

"Reverence for Life"

At a recent clergy meeting we got to discussing the term "reverence for life" as used by Albert Schweitzer. One of the clergy told of hearing a sermon by Howard Thurman at Boston University, in which Thurman pointed out that animal life is ruled by survival of the fittest. The question was raised: Did this mean Thurman was invalidating Schweitzer's proclamation of reverence for life as a spiritual principle? The discussion ended too quickly with no resolution, as other topics claimed the day.

The question kept resurfacing in my mind, however. I realize we have been told that the "law of nature" is survival of the fittest, but is that altogether true? Or is it that when there is no way of intervening with the destructive forces, the fittest survive. Even in nature, when intervention is possible, the strong do sometimes protect the weak. Mother and father animals in some species nurse, nurture, and protect their young. If only the fittest survived, with no other creature reverencing their lives, most species would have died out long ago. The mother lioness may not reverence the life of the baby gazelle, but she does reverence the life of her own cub. Could it not be that both reverence for life and survival of the fittest are "laws of nature"?

There is the other question too: why do we humans have to base our ethical and moral choices on the so-called laws of nature? Even if in the wild the only law is tooth and fang, shouldn't we humans reverence life? As I pondered, I was reading the book, *Happy Is the Land*, by Louise Dickinson Rich, the account of her life in the backwoods of Maine in the 1930s and 40s. She tells of raising a motherless fawn using the same baby formula she was feeding to her infant daughter, Dinah. She writes:

> "*The fawn loved the formula and the bottle. It grew up and was turned loose, finally. I know where Howard picked it up, but what I really think of when I pass that spot is that the first sharing of Dinah's life was with a bit of animation that had no claims of its own. Nature is*

45

ruthless; the fawn should have died. But human nature isn't like that.
We care. I like to remember that before she was old enough to know
what she was doing, Dinah subscribed to the doctrine that the strong
have a responsibility toward the weak."

Now from what I know of both Schweitzer and Thurman, they too subscribed to that doctrine. Despite their flaws, they were very caring people. As I hope, despite our flaws, we are. We all are bitterly aware of how ruthless nature can be, and because of, not in spite of, that ruthlessness, we care. We are well aware that no human life, however fit, would survive long without the care of other humans.

The Christmas story is about that caring, that reverence for life, that belief that the strong have a responsibility toward the weak. Mary, Joseph, Jesus—their story is not one of survival of the fittest. Their story is of reverence for life. Their story is about people caring for other people—everyone from the innkeeper to the wise men, insuring that the most helpless creature in the world, a newborn baby, would survive.

We are always coming up against these two "laws of nature"—survival of the fittest and reverence for life. We need to remember to care, to reverence life, and particularly, to remember the responsibility the strong have towards the weak.

"Nature is ruthless . . . But human nature isn't like that. We care." Is that the truth or wishful thinking? Only in our living can we make it true.

From Kwanzaa to Martin Luther King Day

A few years ago my congregation in Kenosha, Wisconsin, celebrated Kwanzaa by each of us, adults and children, affixing names of African American heroes and ancestors, written on colorful paper, to a black plastic cloth creating a quilt to hang on the sanctuary wall. Some were names I provided copied out of books or typed: Martin Luther King, Jr., Rosa Parks, Whitney Young, Jr., Daisy Bates, Marian Wright Edelman, Colin Powell. Famous African Americans active in the past or present.

Others were names of personal heroes that parishioners wrote down themselves. Some of these were well-known people in Kenosha: Thelma Orr, Mary Lou Mahone, Bill Tompkins, Pastor Olen Arrington, Jr., Adelene Robinson. Some were people known only to the person who wrote the name. All of these I call the everyday heroes.

The name that touched me the most was one of those everyday heroes. Written in a child's scrawl were these words: "My doctor when I broke my arm." Those words evoked a picture of a frightened child and a doctor who must have done more than simply put bones back into place, a doctor who took the time to ease a child's fears, a doctor who healed a child's soul as well as body. A black doctor and a white child.

My heart lifted as I read those words, and I felt hope. Hope that another doctor's dream, the dream of Dr. Martin Luther King, Jr., the dream that people of all colors could live together in peace and joy and love in America is still alive, is happening.

Often I feel despair when I look at America today, for so much of that dream is still a dream. Legal segregation is gone, but segregation still exists. There are bright, shiny schools and there are dingy, tattered schools. There are state-of the art hospitals and there are crowded clinics. The ghetto is still a part of American cities.

In that America we need the hope of the white child who sees her black doctor as a hero. We need the hope of the assemblies of people who gather on Martin Luther King Day to honor his life's work.

Most of all, we need to take up the fabric of Dr. King's dream and weave it into the tapestry of our lives. We need to do his work. We can be the everyday heroes who turn Dr. King's dream into reality. When we make that dream come true, we will be celebrating Dr. Martin Luther King, Jr., every day of our lives. What a celebration it will be!

What Kind of American Are You?

"The thought of America hung before me like a cliff." Tony D'Souza. These words from the novel *Whiteman* by Tony D'Souza were quoted in a New York Times Book Review by Wyatt Mason. The book recounts a young American's life in the African bush village of Tegeso working for Potable Water International. Jack Diaz, the narrator, goes there to change the lives of the Worodougou people. He discovers he is no good at changing their lives. They are much better at changing his. When the time comes to return to America, he is reluctant. "The thought of America hung before me like a cliff."

What about America held him back? Is it the America unaware of its wealth? When Jack arrived in Tegeso, he was surprised to learn the villagers thought him rich. He had been careful to come with only the basics for an American: a transistor radio and tape deck, pricey hiking sandals and equally expensive clothes. His American obliviousness to the villagers' way of life immediately set him apart.

Yet there is also the America of generosity. Shocked by the villagers' assessment of him, he gives them all his possessions. Perhaps thinking it over, he felt guilty of being the patronizing American, the Lord Bountiful, but there is also the understanding American of reciprocity. After he gave away all he had, Jack is showered with gifts, all the necessities of life in Tegeso: a sun hat, a machete, ragged field clothes. He accepts these gifts with real gratitude, saying: "Just as soon as I had been naked among them, I was dressed again."

Is he afraid to return to the America of arrogance and ineptitude? Potable Water International was going to solve water, health and violence problems in various villages. Of the seventeen Americans in the group, at year's end only six remained, and the villages were unchanged. All that hubris come to naught. Yet there is also the America of refreshing honesty and heartfelt caring. When asked by a Belgian banker, how successful he was, Jack Diaz replies he had made no difference. When asked by a villager, why he stayed, he replied, "Something inside me compels me to stay."

The same evening I read that book review, Paul Rusesabagina, the real life hotel manager hero of Hotel Rwanda, was interviewed on PBS about his autobiography, *An Ordinary Man*, Rusesabagina said to the interviewer that he was an ordinary man who saved people by ordinary measures and that others can do the same. The interviewer did not seem convinced. Jack Diaz, the fictional ordinary man, would probably agree with the interviewer. Yet in his book D'Souza represents Jack, an ordinary man, showing the village people the other side of the American cliff of arrogance and greed, the side where ordinary people help each other in small ways, and when called upon, in the largest ways.

In his interview, Paul Rusesabagina called upon the ordinary people of the world to help the people of Darfur. Many of us do what we can both with our money and our letters of concern to government officials. We are trying to be the kind of Americans we are most proud of being—those who help others. There will always be Darfurs. We are all ordinary Americans: the question is on which side of the cliff do we live? How will we respond when the Darfurs call us?

Deliver Us From Evil—

An Easter Message

"Turn my eyes away from what my human weakness cannot as yet understand and therefore cannot bear to think about"

Teilhard de Chardin,
Roman Catholic theologian

I read mysteries as an escape. I like mysteries set in interesting places particularly. The local color allows me to armchair travel. Often, as in the Tony Hillerman mysteries of the Navaho detectives, I learn about other cultures; sometimes profoundly as in the explanation of the Navaho belief true justice brings the world back into balance which sometimes means forgoing punishment in the white man's sense of that word. Other lessons are not profound but are pleasurable, as in the many recipes that the cozier mysteries often include in their pages. Mostly there is the satisfaction that the mystery is solved, the villain is caught and justice triumphs. But sometimes, a mystery writer has a harsher but truer message, that whatever justice has been achieved, the evil has not been stopped—that the evil is systematic in society. A silent question screams from the book: Is there no hope for humanity?

Such was the case with Donna Leon's 1995 Venetian mystery, *Death and Judgment*. I closed the book and covered my face with my hands. My stomach churned. The day was warm, but I was cold: chilled to the heart by the evil uncovered and the knowledge that this is not an isolated evil but one that occurs every day throughout our world, and yes, here in America.

The evils the book exposes are sexual slavery and murder—the preying on poor women by global sex traffickers. This modern day slavery is getting more press lately (12 years after Leon's book was published). We are hearing a call for us to work against this terrible injustice. There are news articles and scholarly studies. But all you need to wake yourself up to the need for action is read this engrossing, harrowing mystery novel.

Easter is the time of colored eggs, the rebirth of spring, songs of joyous resurrection, and the time to remember the radical love that Jesus taught—the love that commands us not to turn our eyes away from what we cannot understand—but to open our eyes and the eyes of the world. To cry out: deliver us from evil. And then to work to do so.

Sometimes Peace Happens

In preparation for a sermon on peace, I read *Hiroshima Diary* by Dr. Michihiko Hachiya. At the end of the book an American soldier asks Dr. Hachiya how he feels about the bombing. The doctor replies that as a Buddhist he is resigned to the suffering and thankful that he and his family survived. "I can't share your feelings," the American replied. "If I were you, I'd sue the country." Dr. Hachiya was amazed. It was totally incomprehensible to him that a person would advise someone to sue the government. The American was out of line to the Japanese.

On the other hand, I once had an English friend who told me that what he liked about Americans was that we complained. "So much more useful than our British stiff-upper lip-suffer-in-silence attitude. That's why I love it when there are Americans on our bus tours," he said. "You complain for all of us."

Nowadays in the United States, litigation seems to have run amok, veneration for anyone is at an all time low, and complaining has developed into a cultural necessity. Don't you love being asked in interviews—"What's your weakness?"—thus, compelling us to complain about ourselves! It is good for us to remember the value of complaining—emperor worship is certainly more dangerous than president trashing, and no one should ever put up with real abuse. However, perhaps, as a nation, we need also to remember the value of honest admiration, helpful counsel, kind words in season, forgiveness for human failings, and acknowledgement that, as the poet Robert Burns (translated into English) wrote, "sometimes the best laid plans of mice and men go astray," and the best response is to be gracious. Sometimes peace happens because we don't complain!

Finding Nemo—A Spiritual

Lesson from a Grandson

"Fish are friends, not food," my grandson says to me with utter seriousness. "Yes," I answer, wondering does this mean I must now become a complete vegetarian?

My grandson received his wisdom from *Finding Nemo*, a movie he watches religiously. I say religiously since he has obviously taken to heart one of the messages of the movie: all creatures should be friends to each other, and friends don't eat each other. He has not become a vegetarian, which would be to follow the message literally. Perhaps he will, and perhaps he won't. What I hope is that he will remember and live all his life the spiritual message of this first religious experience: treat all of life with kindness; betray no one by willfully hurting them.

Many folks keep their children from watching TV and movies afraid that TV will rot children's minds, kill their imaginations and turn them into couch potatoes. I too worry about TV and videos. Yet as my grandson and I made jellyfish out of plastic bags and swam around the room with them, as he danced with the dancers on television's High Five, and then ignored the TV to set up his train set, I realized that children may have more innate sense than we give them credit for. He seemed quite capable of tuning out the TV. Even more, he liked the new trick I taught him: turning off the TV with the words: Magic! Quiet!

What is important is not where our children get their messages, but what messages are they getting? And how do these messages change their lives? It is crucial to talk with and listen to our children to find out how they interpret the messages they hear. It is crucial that we give them messages we consider important. It is crucial we play with them using imagination to integrate messages into their subconscious, and finally, most crucial we must show them how to practice the messages in their lives.

Perhaps we still eat fish, but we thank the fish for giving us nourishment, reminding us that fish are friends. Perhaps, we even become complete vegetarians. Beyond the literal meaning, we help children understand the symbolic messages of friendship, kindness, loyalty to all people in our lives. All creatures are our friends becomes our practice. We are all here to find Nemo.

Children's Stories and Spirituality—

Water Babies, Darwin and Me

While researching a sermon on Charles Darwin, I learned that the 19th century minister and writer Charles Kingsley's children's book *Water Babies* had been inspired by Darwin and his evolutionary theory. *Water Babies* had been one of my favorite childhood books. It is the story of the chimney sweep, Tom, who falls into the river and turns into a water baby.

My parents spent a summer of trepidation as they watched me spending longer and longer times swimming underwater. They feared I might take the book too literally and somehow contrive to drown myself. Unfortunately they didn't reveal their fears until I was grown-up; at which point I laughed at them and said, "But I knew the story was make-believe. I was playing!" Sometimes it is good to talk to your child if you're worried.

I decided to reread the book to find out where Darwin came in, since I had no recollection of being exposed to the theory of evolution through Kingsley's tale. I was disappointed to find that Kingsley slurred the Irish and Americans; in fact, the only nationalities he approved were the English and Scottish. However, either my mother skipped these passages or they didn't register with me as a child. What did register was the delight of a child living in the water, and the story of spiritual growth as Tom evolves from abused chimney sweep to cheeky water baby to caring human man. He learns his lessons from a trinity of water women spirits: Mrs. Bedonebyasyoudid, Mrs. Doasyouwouldbedoneby, and Mother Carey.

He learns the Golden Rule from the first two and then Mother Carey assigns to him his final task for his transformation which is "to do the thing he does not like." Tom must seek out his former abuser, the master sweep Grimes, and help Grimes find redemption. Along the way Tom meets a giant who upsets the populaces of various imaginary domains by smashing up their temples to uncover obscure specimens. As an adult, I recognized Darwin; as a child, the giant was just another fantastical and amusing creature.

There is an exercise in self-analysis in which people are asked to tell the story that they most loved as a child. They need not remember it perfectly because the idea is that however you remember the story is the way in which it influenced you. When first asked the question, I replied *The Princess and the Goblins* by George MacDonald. I remembered it as a story about a princess (and MacDonald tells us that every little girl is a princess) guided by a mysterious godmother who gives her a ball of invisible yarn that will always lead her home. The princess in company with a miner's son and her ball of yarn rids the land of the goblins.

The second part of the exercise is to figure out what your story taught you that you carried into your adult life. For me the answer was: I learned there is a spirit helping us which gives us a lifeline to follow to lead us right in times of danger and that to accomplish larger goals we need to make friendships across class lines. Thinking about *Water Babies* in the same way, what I internalized were the joy of freedom, the importance of the Golden Rule, and the fact that sometimes we must do what we do not want to do.

What were your favorite children's stories? How have their messages resonated in your life? What children's stories are you sharing with your children and grandchildren? Take some time to remember and ponder—you'll learn something about yourself. And you'll definitely think even more carefully about what books to give the children in your life.

Good reading to you all.

Hair: A Story of Two Cultures

My son Hans e-mailed me from Japan that he had shaved off his beard because "it was frightening the ladies (and the men)." I immediately e-mailed a minister colleague who collects stories on hair conflicts, saying to her that this was perhaps the first instance of hair being seen as a tool of the oppressor. Usually hair stories are about the person with unusual hair being oppressed, becoming the object of ridicule, having employment terminated or in general, being victimized. Now, I suppose had my son refused to shave his beard, all the above could have happened to him.

Perhaps if those frightened by his hirsuteness had curtly told him, "No beards, that's the rule," he might have rebelled, or reluctantly shaved while inwardly feeling oppressed. However, whoever broached the subject did so in a manner that appealed to his sense of chivalry—a gentleman does not knowingly manifest behavior or appearance that would frighten ladies (or even other gentlemen). Although the very terms lady and gentleman are no longer considered politically correct in this country, apparently the concept has not vanished in Japan, or even in my son's consciousness since he responded by doing the gentlemanly thing—shaving!

By way of explanation of why the ladies and gents in Japan might find his beard frightening, I can offer only two suggestions: one, Japan is a society in which few men have hairy beards and sideburns; two, my son has brown-blond hair, but his beard and sideburns are red. This dichotomy of color between top of head and chin may be just too disconcerting in a country where all the people have one color hair—period. After all, isn't it enough that his students are expected to get used to this fellow with hair the color of wet noodles; to expect them to concentrate while also staring at a lower face bristling with a fiery red beard and sideburns risks boggling their minds. His beard might well arouse in his students fearful visions of a teacher with a piratical ancestry rather than the staid Yankee millers or the devout Eastern European rabbis whose genes in actuality dot his DNA. (Although I must admit to a few seafaring folk among the Yankees, virtuous sailors or pirates, I am not sure.)

The fact remains that the hair issue was easily resolved because of the manner in which the appeal was voiced: "Please, you are scaring us"—instead of "Conform or else we will make you suffer." Did they really find the beard scary or simply unaesthetic? Was he frightening them or just culturally out-of-bounds? Were they genuinely appealing to his compassion or were they asking him to follow the Japanese way in which the individual puts the needs of the group first? Was it a simple manipulative tactic—a guilt trip?

In American society, we would have started petitions for the teacher's right to have a beard. We might have initiated a consciousness-raising group to help the students face their intolerance of beards and learn the truth about bicolor hirsuteness. Was Hans un-American to surrender so easily? Chivalry is dead, right?

Sometimes, sometimes not. Why not take the best from both societies? Sometimes we should cut our hair to suit our fellows, and sometimes we should flaunt our locks to celebrate our individuality. Maturity is knowing there is a choice, and taking the time and consideration to make that choice wisely.

The Impermanence of Perfection

In a recent issue of *Echoes*, a magazine chronicling life in northern Maine, writer Torrey Sylvester told of winning a cribbage game from his dad with the perfect score of twenty-nine. Scores of twenty-nine are extremely rare—often a once in a lifetime event.

Cribbage, Sylvester explained, was invented four hundred years ago by an English math professor and poet, Sir John Suckling. It is a game that requires a mathematical mind, which explains why I have never become a cribbage player. I do, however, somewhere among the family treasures, have a cribbage board. An oblong of varnished pine dotted with holes, the board possesses a simple beauty, but I keep it for reasons of sentiment, not aesthetics. It reminds me of my dad.

I don't know if Dad ever achieved a twenty-nine in cribbage, but he certainly had fun playing. On a boat trip down the St. Lawrence River, he played with a Canadian as whimsical as he, who claimed to be the Unofficial North American Cribbage Champion. Dad won the unofficial title from him. Both men enjoyed a victory glass of scotch. Winner and loser were equally happy, taking my dad's victory as proof that they were both worthy opponents—both champions. Although perhaps not quite the champions they claimed to be, there was a twinkle in their eyes that led us all to beware taking their titles seriously. Likewise when Torrey Sylvester scored his perfect twenty-nine, everyone including his dad celebrated. The triumph was not of one man over another but of both over the odds of the game.

In the Olympics perfect scores are almost as rare as in cribbage. For most players winning the gold means everything; there is little joy in silver or bronze, and none in defeat. Even at the Olympics though there are players who say with seeming honesty, "I'm just glad to be here. To be able to compete at this level." After all, to be a competitor in the Olympics means you are better at what you do than most of the world. All Olympians are champions.

To be that good usually means you love the sport. Slicing into the pool from the high diving board, swirling across the ice, twisting cleanly over the high jump, racing down the track—the thrill of the sport is the joy.

Sometimes that love of the sport preempts the rivalry. Sometimes on those rare occasions when the perfect score is rung up, losers enthusiastically hug the winner. Sometimes the winner is both exultant and humble, professing that grace and luck played as much a part in the winning as skill. Even the best cribbage player needs good cards to win; even the best runner can stumble in the wind. The real winners in life know just how close the line is between winning and losing. They know the impermanence of perfection. When everything comes together in triumph, they celebrate with joy and give thanks that this time the winds were in their favor, the winning cards were dealt them. And what of the so-called losers? When they do less than the world expected, some of them have the gumption and true grace of figure skater Michelle Kwan who replied, "I didn't lose the gold medal. I won the silver!"

The reality is most of us only get a few perfect scores in life, a few silver medals, a few A's; yet we keep on doing what we love, hoping that it is good enough, and usually it is. The less than perfect dive of a professional diver makes me shiver with its elegance; the singer who will never make it to Carnegie Hall lifts my heart with her song; the preacher who will never be listed among the top ten preachers in the country can send me home inspired for the week ahead. Perfect scores are usually once in a lifetime events. The reality is how good an imperfect performance can be. For that, we should be truly thankful!

Resurrection

I have a lovely pink conch shell. When I hold it to my ear, I can hear the echo of the ocean—or so my grandmother told me, that magically, mysteriously the sound of the sea was caught in the shell's whorls—as if somehow there were a teeny beach hidden in the innermost circle of the conch's trumpet: a land beyond, unreachable to us giants, a land we can only hear in the echo.

The conch shell was a mystery from nature and a solace to the soul of a child. It was as if the shell were whispering a secret from eternity: "Here is all that is left of me, calcified beauty, kidnapped from the ocean, set upon a shelf in a village sitting room, once a living being tossed in the turbulent sea, now a knick-knack, a dust-catcher, a souvenir of a summer day, trivialized . . . until a child holds me to her ear and hears eternity surging, the ringing, singing, windy whooshing of the sea issuing forth from my pink and pearly chambers."

Whatever the scientific explanation—for it was explained to me—I could never remember the science of it; what I remembered was the mystery, the story that the ocean was in the shell. And what I knew then and know now is the truth—that the ocean is in the shell, as the shell was once in the ocean—that no matter how far we are from the source, what we love echoes in our lives.

And after death, when we, like the being that once inhabited the conch, leave our shells, we too leave an echo behind. Resurrection echoes in our lives from all whom we have loved; if we but lift the conch to our ears, we will hear.

Blithe Spirit

When I was a high school drama coach, I directed a production of Noel Coward's *Blithe Spirit*. Doing research on the play, I learned that it was one of Winston Churchill's favorites. The play ran in London during World War II, and Churchill would often slip out of his office and drop in to see if not the whole play, at least a scene or two. The play was as popular with the English public as with Churchill. Why, I wondered, would people who lived in fear of imminent death day and night, people engaged in the momentous task of fighting a staggering war, spend the little free time they had at this superficial, albeit funny, comedy?

The obvious answers are escape and relief. The elegant mannered characters, the witty repartee, the civilized drawing room setting of the 1930s, a throwback to a time when Londoners could drink their cocktails without fear of air raids—all of this provided an oasis where for a few hours one could forget and live again in a time when all was well. However, as I started working on the play a light dawned, *Blithe Spirit* is more than just a drawing room comedy evoking nostalgia for the safety of years past. It is a comedy about death.

Elvira, the dead first wife, materializes and wreaks havoc with her mischievous charm. Elvira is impish, flirtatious, sarcastic, infuriating, delightful—no different in death than she was in life. Her character has not improved during her seven years in the afterlife, neither has her attractiveness diminished. She is in fact everyone's best fantasy of a ghost—a blithe spirit telling folks that death is just another version of life. Here, I am Elvira proclaims, as annoying and glamorous as ever.

It occurred to me that the wartime audience must have experienced the play very differently from the postwar audiences. The play is always entertaining, but for that wartime audience in the midst of the ever-present reality of death, it gave them the special gift of laughing at death. Their worst fears suddenly were embodied as a delightful woman in gray chiffon with sparkles in her hair. For the few hours of the play life and death intermingled without grief or fear.

The play was just a brief respite—the audiences returned to face the reality of war—but the laughter gave them the needed healing to continue. Sometimes fear causes us to isolate ourselves, or to obsess, thinking we have to concentrate only on solving our problems. Yet in war, Churchill took time out to join with others in laughter. We need to pray, to sing, to be with those we love, to take action, to savor the preciousness of life, to understand the seriousness of the problems we face. But we also need to follow the example of Winston Churchill, and in the midst of a world filled with fear and trembling, take time out to laugh—to laugh at even our worst fears. Laughter is a saving grace—try it.

A Sigh of Relief—From December

to January

I feel as if I am skidding down a long snow-covered hill called December. Or perhaps it is more like falling down Alice's rabbit hole, for around me float the amazing flotsam and jetsam of my December life. As I descend candles flicker on all sides—Hanukkah candles, Advent Candles, Christmas Candles, Kwanzaa candles . . . don't forget the candles! And lists—meeting that was on second Fridays now on third Thursday, choose carols for Christmas, make an elephant for Hanukkah play. Oh, yes, and then there's the little matter of my own family—they still appreciate some gifts, you know! Can you make the caroling someone calls out as we meet floating down the December rabbit hole. Can you? Will you? Have you? . . . Stop the world I want to get off!

Breathe . . . Thich Nhat Hanh reminds me.

One thing at a time my mother tells me. All you can do is the best you can.

What's the use of the fuss if you don't enjoy yourself? That's advice from my own teenage self—it was in response to my first bout of stage fright. I got through the play fine but was too worried about messing up to enjoy acting. I had an epiphany then—acting is something you don't do unless you want to, therefore, no use acting unless you enjoy it. I decided to let go of the fear, and to concentrate on relishing being on stage. Once that happened, all was well.

Now as I skid into January, landing kerplunk at the bottom of the rabbit hole, I remind myself I love the turbulence of December, the whirl of holidays, the celebrating of Absolutely Everything. Just as I love the sweet thud of landing in January.

January is simplicity. No more ornaments, no more tree. Poinsettia's off to Poinsettia Vacationland, dark and solitary. Narcissus, hyacinth, amaryllis, harbingers of spring in our austere January rooms. The comforting peaceful healing of rooms swept clear of the clutter that cheered us so in December. Now we can sit and remember the holidays over a quiet cup of tea, look out on branches decorated only with snow, through windows etched with frost. Nature's beauty in January can make us gasp after an ice storm when the world glitters and clatters, rainbows sparkling suddenly from the whiteness, reminding us that white is really all the colors of the prism.

"To paint snow," an artist once told me, "be very sparing of white, snow is many-colored." The artist looked at the snow with the sharpness and slowness that saw what was hidden to the swiftly observing eye. In January as life slows, we can slow too and look with the sharp eyes of the artist at the world around us. We can see the colors darting out from snow, frost and ice; sunlight and moon glow creating nature's special effects.

In the simplicity of whiteness, the simplicity of light, in the pristine starkness of the New Year, we can see what we missed in December's turbulent decoration. We can see the rainbow in the snow, the pink sunrise over the harbor, the evergreen tree in the forest ornamented with pinecones and snow. We are freed by the simplicity to see anew the world around us. We are freed to set out afresh on journeys of discovery.

The simplicity of January energizes our fallow imaginations from which bursts out: the idea that sets fingers flying over the keys, paint brush flashing over the canvas, a note soaring into an untraversed octave. May your January start you on a new journey of the heart, whether it be the simple planting of a hyacinth to gladden your winter home or the trip of a thousands of miles to fulfill your life's dream. Look into the simplicity and discover your essentials.

Why Can't the Rest of the Year

Be More Like February?

February as far as I am concerned is the only orderly month of the year. February is so precise: four weeks exactly; twenty-eight days from start to finish. You can depend on February. No worrying about whether there are thirty or thirty-one days, except every four years when you have the maverick 29th, but even that is okay because so much publicity surrounds that errant day it is impossible to forget. Why can't the rest of the year be so precisely ordered? Something to do with some pope in the Middle Ages changing the calendar. Useless to protest against that now. We are stuck with eleven erratic months and one simple, clear-cut month, dear old February.

So it is with life itself. Most of it chaotic, hard to hang onto, its dates and days always changing. One month the 7th is a Saturday; the next, a Friday. Christmas hops all through the week, and though Easter remains true to Sunday it has no allegiance as to month, traveling throughout March and April like a ping pong ball, dependent on the moon to call its shots—a rather strange way to run a supposedly non-pagan religious holiday, but hey, I, a Unitarian Universalist, can hardly complain!

But dear old February, we can set our clocks by. The mighty groundhog will see its shadow or not every February 2. Valentine's Day is February 14, no matter what day of the week. Valentine refuses to be coerced by the government into becoming a Monday holiday. Abraham Lincoln's birthday is still February 12 and Washington's the 22nd, but here's where the rot sets in and disorder looms for government and department stores have rounded the two days into one and made the third Monday suffice for two of the greatest leaders of this country. Worse the American way of celebrating these men, who sacrificed so much for their country, is to spend the day plunking down their images to buy mattresses, cars, and Ipods all at Presidents Day Sales prices. If we are finally learning that Martin Luther King Day should be spent honoring Dr. King's memory, might we not do the same for Lincoln and Washington? Do our children even know what virtuosos the young Lincoln and Washington were with their axes? Do they realize what those stories taught? Hard work and honesty—the virtues of an orderly society. Instead we teach our children the virtue of shoving their way to the front of the line at Walmart's. Actually, I hope you don't teach that lesson, but it sure is in the communal ether.

So what can we do, to bask in the simple orderliness of February and keep ourselves above the fray of those who would demean our greatest presidents by turning them into hucksters?

Here's my recipe: Listen to the groundhog on the 2nd, knowing full well that whatever that pudgy rodent sees there will be six more weeks of winter, but it's sweet of him to try to make us feel that spring could actually arrive in February. On the 3rd buy your valentines, and send out at least ten to friends and family to cheer them up with your love on what could well be a blizzardy day. On the 12th recall Abraham Lincoln's words: "With malice towards none, with charity towards all"—and forgive someone. On the 14th tell at least one creature you love them, be it dog, housefly, or husband. On the 22nd tell the truth about any cherry trees you have mistreated and make amends. Finally, on that Monday when you're supposed to go out and buy, buy, buy; stay home and save, save, save!

Hooray for February!

April by the Sea—A Hopeful Month

April is a-swirl in holidays and holy days. Passover, Easter, Eostre, Spring, Earth Day, Holocaust Remembrance Day, Patriot's Day in Massachusetts also coupled with Marathon Day. It's enough to make us dizzy, even if we're not celebrating or solemnizing each one. All of this and April itself—that month of sudden heat and just as sudden snow, of crocus picked by mittened hands, and snow shoveled in tee shirts.

T.S. Eliot, not apparently liking such extremes and surprises, called April "the cruelest month." Not me, after slogging through March, nothing April brings can upset me. April is "the hopeful month" to me. April calls out: new life, new hope.

April jumps us forward into the long, light evenings of spring and summer. April rejoices us with daffodils, crocus, tulips. Why should we mind that sometimes April heightens their intensity with a fringe of snow, for April's snows melt away in a morning's sunshine. The daffodils, crocus, and tulips rebound dazzling from their encounter with the snow's last grace note

Our hearts lift as the sweet, salt breeze off the sea whispers: "Come down to the wharf, to the beach, to the brine. It's time for shovels and buckets, for sails and oars, for dips and dodges in the waves, for toes wiggling in the sand. It's time for the sea breeze to tickle your fancy and take you away from computer and stove and down to the sea's edge in delight." April swirls and twirls, teases and tickles, tosses us to our knees and sweeps us off our feet, but April never bores us. April laughs and we laugh too. Life surges up in our veins and we set out anew to see the greening of the land, to breathe the vigor of the sea, and to feel the warm, gentle sunshine invade our bodies and souls.

Celebrate and solemnize those April holidays and holy days you hold dear. And then open your doors and dance with April. Do the two-step on your porch, bow to a daffodil in your garden and fly a kite in the dancing April wind. Feel hope soar in your heart. If you see me on the way, tip your hat and give me a turn at the kite,

April in New Hampshire—

The River Calls

As I sat at my desk without a thought in my head, I considered sending in as my column these words: THINK FOR YOURSELF THIS MONTH. (As if Unitarian Universalists ever do anything but think for themselves.) I could hear the phone ringing: Hey, tell us something new for a change. If you only have five words of advice can't you be more innovative than that! What do we pay you for—go out there and get an idea.

A writer friend of mine was once asked, "Where do you get your ideas?" She said, "Oh, I just go pick them like flowers." Ah, were it only so! I could nurture a Garden of Theological Concepts with a Border of Pastoral Thoughts surrounding a Fishpond of Administrative Advice, and a patch of Platitudes, Euphemisms, Unitarian Universalist Jokes, Assorted Trivia and Wisdom for All Occasions. I could stroll out, gather my thoughts quite literally, and transform them into prose bouquets each month.

Alas, I have no such garden, so what can I offer you this month—April? I can tell you the truth that April often comes in like a lion and out like a lamb, like her brother March, so don't start grumbling about the weather until April 25. April is the month taxes are due as taxes are due every April, so don't act surprised. April is church canvass month, as usual, but remember unlike taxes, you don't have to pay your pledge in a lump sum. You have all year to pay it. True, there's no hope of a Pledge Refund, but you will continue to enjoy worship, religious education for your children, suppers, music, food, inspirational and intellectual talk in small groups, book groups, coffee hour, etc. So count your blessings.

All of which is to say you'll get no sympathy from me if April brings with it gale winds, snow, and its usual outgo of money and promise of support for our church community. Don't bother to complain to me about April's ills! However, if you'd like to share your joy over the first crocus, daffodil, robin, the first day when the sun and breeze tantalize, I'd be happy to put on my walking shoes and hike down the river trail with you. The waters of the Nubanusit are foaming and frothing. The new green is on the trees. Let's walk!

The Lovely Month of May

May, the lovely month of May. Here I sit half way in April, but on this day, the sun is warm, the sky is blue, and May seems a real possibility! In my office window, brilliant red tulips tilt toward the sun, a gift from a parishioner, who popped in my office with a smile and a gift of flowers. "May is a'coming," the tulips announce. "Soon you'll see us in gardens." Oh, what bliss, my imagination soars: purple, pink, gold, lavender, white, red, orange tulips sprouting, springing, sprinkling Peterborough with satiny color, waking up the earth so long asleep under its white coverlet. Daffodils dappling our world gold, but first will be the crocuses shouting out triumphantly, "It's time. Come along the rest of you. Up and at 'em! May's coming."

Forsythia, lilacs, the whole chorus line of spring is in the wings, about to make their entrance. Surprises too, what are those green stalks in my garden patch? I could call the parish gardener who planted them so expertly, ask her what they'll turn into, but no, I think I'll just wait for May to tickle the stalks upward and reveal their true identity. Around the corner of my deck, freed from Mt. Snow, the rosebush another parishioner planted with me last summer struggles to maintain its poise. Battered by wintering, its branches are scrawny and browned, but undefeated it turns towards the sun. Will there be roses this summer, sweet-scented briar roses?

May is promise, surprise, expectation. May is generosity run rampant as the treasures hidden in the earth burst out in glory. May is a reminder that, yes, some gifts do keep on giving. Tulips bloom that were planted on crisp autumn days years ago by folks departed to other climes, even to other worlds. In Bangor, Maine, do the tulip bulbs I ordered with such discernment, and planted with gusto amidst a plethora of mud, herald spring to people I will never know? I hope so. It is good to think I left behind a trail of tulips. Just as it is good to be greeted by the blossoms of last summer's plantings. Good to hope that someday after I am gone, these flowers will cheer a fellow traveler I may never know.

May reminds us of the generosity of gardeners, who plant not for one season, but for the cycle of many generations, not for themselves alone, but for those who come after, whoever they may be. Digging and planting, weeding and watering, putting their faith into seeds and bulbs, these gardeners bequeath gifts of beauty into the world. We cannot all be gardeners of the earth, but we can all be gardeners of the spirit, planting and nurturing gifts of beauty in our world, gifts that delight, gifts that sustain, gifts we pass on to those who follow us. What blooms in your garden for the generations ?

The Magic of June

June . . . a magical name . . . conjuring up visions of Paradise remembered from childhood—School's Out. Summer's In. Or as we used to chant: "No more pencils, no more books, no more teacher's dirty looks!"

You would think that school was drudgery and teachers, monsters, when in fact I enjoyed school and heartily cared for my elementary school teachers.

Yet, there was still that wonderful feeling of release that came with June—the realization that utter freedom was just around the corner . . . long days at the beach stretching into twilight evenings of hide-and-seek, of lolling in canvas chairs singing, giggling, solving the world's problems, drinking tonic (this being New England), a swarm of kids with adults somewhere off in the shadows, near enough to be called if a spat turned into a fight.

One of the hardest things about growing up is that most of us lose that cycle of summer freedom. Instead, we are leashed into jobs that give us a few weeks to a month off. Teachers and Unitarian Universalist ministers are among the fortunates who still get to rejoice each June as freedom beckons. Although I do not chant: "No more sermons, no more books, no more parishioners' dirty looks!" I enjoy my ministry, and heartily care for my parishioners. But, I would be less than honest if I did not admit that the release from deadlines—and the thought of having a row of balmy days for lolling in chairs made of whatever stuff lawn chairs are made of nowadays—is breathtakingly inviting.

Iced tea, sometimes even wine, replaces tonic now-a-summers. I am looking forward even to a few cream sodas. I'll be one of the adults off in the shadows ready to be called into saving action if necessary—although one discovers, when one grows up, that the adults are actually having some fun themselves, talking, even sometimes giggling and singing—and still trying to solve the problems of the world. It almost seems possible that we could as we sip our cold drinks and watch the red sun sink sleepily into the golden sea, and the stars shimmer awake.

I did learn a secret trick those summers when vacation time was restricted to one or two weeks. Probably you know it, but just in case you've forgotten: we all get a little extra freedom in June, July and August—the freedom of summer evenings when we are graced with those special hours of summer light. What a gift after being shut inside all day. My heart would lift as four o'clock announced: freedom! How I loved those long summer evenings—it was as if each day were two days—one for work and one for play. I could do a lot of lolling and swimming and giggling with my friends and family in a summer evening.

Henry James said the most beautiful words in the English language are "summer afternoon'—for the working class (except for those on night shift), I'd say the most beautiful words are "summer evening." Instead of feeling cheated out of freedom, we can all rejoice in the wonderful treasure of summer.

Alleluia!

Summer—Can't We Just Play?

All the summers of my childhood, all we did was play. No summer camp, no summer school, no formal lessons of any sort, we just played. My own children were not so advantaged. They had years of summer nursery school, summer camp, summer outdoor programs, until finally one summer they pleaded: "Please do we have to? Can't we just play?"

Happily, it was a downtime in the high tech industry, and I was able to take a sabbatical summer with money I'd saved. I was happy to have a chance to just be with my boys. At nine and ten sometimes they went their merry ways to play with friends; more often together, we swam at the beach and quarry, scrambled over rocks and hunted crabs. There was still a schoolyard then, and in the evenings, the neighborhood children played scrub baseball and hide and seek, until their mothers called them home.

I think of this because I recently read an article about how over-scheduled children are nowadays, how they have so little time just to play. I think of a poignant moment from the PBS series *Frontier House* when the little boy summed up what he learned from playing with the other children in the wilderness in one word: "Imagination."

I think of two fathers in Kenosha, Wisconsin, who every summer Friday night for over ten years played softball with any neighborhood kids who showed up (boys and girls). No coaching, no uniforms, just playing. (One of the dads admitted ruefully that when they started playing the dads had to be careful not to be too skilled. As the years went by, their sons outbatted and outran them. Such is life!)

The games were the perfect merging of kids playing alone and adults playing with kids because the adults remembered to be kids—to play the game for the fun of playing. Winning truly wasn't important in those games. Important as winning can be in life, we also need to teach our children that life is about more than winning; life is more often about enjoying life together. So whether you are ninety-five or five, I advise living summer slowly, lazily, spending time with those you love in places you love, letting the sun warm you, and the breeze tickle your face, and whenever you can—play with your children. If you can, take a sabbatical summer, and just be.

The Preciousness of Now!

"Tell us one memorable experience you had this summer," the chair of our committee asked. There were so many wonderful moments in my summer vacation, how to choose one. Yet the afternoon that came to my mind was a rainy day in Rockport, Massachusetts, my hometown. My son, Aram, and I were visiting with my brother, my niece and her four little boys. It was a soggy, gray day—not a beach day, the uninitiated might say. A good day, my niece Amy decided for a trek to Bearskin Neck to outfit the boys with the hooded sweatshirts that were their present heart's desire. So off we all trooped together, the three older boys aged eight and down, arrayed in yellow slickers and brandishing (yes, brandishing) umbrellas. The three adults sedately carried our umbrellas. The baby was protected from the rain in his pram. As we marched along, some neighbors came to their door, "Make way for ducklings," someone called out with glee.

The boys proceeded to stomp in every puddle and to stand under every rainspout, declaring rapturously, "Terrible storm!" The rain pranced on their umbrellas. We grown-ups ran interference as the boys, umbrellas amok, plunged into the summer crowd. The new sweatshirts purchased and immediately adorning the dynamic trio, it was obviously too soon to abandon the glories of rain. After all, now the boys had hoods as well as umbrellas. We paraded down the village street to the deserted beach, the rain now a foggy dampness, wind rippling the waters, but ah, a misty, moisty day on the beach is a joy. No radios, no suntan lotion, no picking one's way through infestations of towels—the beach to ourselves, a time to race and riot, to revel in sand and sea and gusty Atlantic air.

A time for me to rejoice in the present—rejoice in my niece, now a mother of great love, humor and common sense—rejoice in these children, chattering away in English accents (for they live in England); these children pulling us into the joy of living in the present when each moment glitters, when life is. A time for me to rejoice also in the past, the memories of so many summer days on the beach with my two sons, the sand castles, the crab hunts, the rock climbing—as well as the battles when one son tired of sun and sea bellowed to go home, and the other relentless in his pursuit of yet another adventure bellowed to stay. A time to rejoice in my adult son, the beach lover, now grown, beside me on this present-day afternoon, grinning at the next generation of boys' antics.

Wet and soggy, we trundled home to warmth and storybooks. "Terrible storm," the boys chorused under the rainspouts. "Terrible storm," we adults chorused back. For there was no terror in the storm, there was only the beauty of gentle rain, the warmth of fuzzy new sweatshirts, the protection of rollicking umbrellas, and the comfort of being family together. We, who are so often separated, know the preciousness of our afternoon together. This was a time of small, sweet blessing, when we glimpsed love whole and knew how blessed we are: a perfectly ordinary afternoon of great joy.

I hope your life has been as blessed with such "terrible storm" days, puddle plopping, umbrella bobbing, the laughter of children ringing in the air reminding you of the Preciousness of Now!

A Harvest Pilgrimage

October was Apple Month when I was growing up. On October 12th, our whole family would go on an Apple Pilgrimage. With my mother at the helm of our 1938 Chevy—a car that lasted well into the 1950s and had a running board, a luxury gone forever, we'd be off. My father, who had never learned to drive, was beside my mother in the front seat. He was the official navigator. My grandmother, looking like Queen Victoria in her most dowagerly augustness, ruled in the back seat, establishing order between my brother and me. Off we sailed over the fall-glorious hills on our Holy Pilgrimage to Rowley, Mass., and Joe Dodge's Orchard.

Joe was a distant cousin of my mother's, and only his apples and his cider were good enough—the genuine article. MacIntoshes, of course, crisp, sweet and juicy. Those Mac's tasted as if all of the sun and wind and sharpness of a New England autumn had been rolled up in a red ball and polished to a shine that no Adam or Eve could resist.

My parents and grandmother would gossip with the Dodges while my brother and I stuffed ourselves on the fresh doughnuts and cider. Then we'd load up the baskets of apples and kegs of cider and drive home through the gold and red maples of October, dreaming of the pleasure we'd have for the next few weeks as we crunched our way through those sumptious apples and drank the cider that would get more and more zippy (my mother's terminology) as the weeks wore on.

Those family trips were pilgrimages, holy in the Emersonian transcendental sense in which the everyday becomes sacred. An ordinary family event was made sacred because it was ritualized, always done on a certain day, always with all of us together, always the same purchases, always with the air of excitement and joy. It was a pilgrimage that was a recognition of the sweet blessing of the harvest-time.

I don't remember how many years we kept it up or when we stopped. In memory now those trips are fixed as moments in eternity, always there, and on those rare occasions when I bite into a perfect MacIntosh nowadays, I can close my eyes and be back nestling beside my grandmother in that old Chevy biting into the original Mac. A gift of a good family ritual can last forever.

Even just a once-in-a-lifetime good day can serve. With my own boys I remember only one such October day that still stands out as magical. We went with friends on an apple picking expedition on a perfect sunlit day. The trees were laden with apples like Christmas trees with ornaments. My boys were used to apples coming in plastic bags—to pick them off the trees with their own hands and fill the baskets to overflowing, to be even just for one afternoon, harvesters, made it a day of great adventure. A day to treasure in memory. At least in mine.

Perhaps to the boys, now men, the memory is not so romantic, but I hope that someday the recollection of apple picking will push them out the door away from TV and computer and off to the orchards with their offspring to create another day for eternity.

And you what are your pilgrimages, your special days? If you don't have any, it is time to create some!

November's Gifts

November in New England is the time of the turning of the year. October is glorious with color. We rejoice in crisp, sunny days and survive the rainy days, omens of the gray November that threatens in our minds. We know one morning we will wake up and the trees will be bare. The one red leaf that tantalized by hanging on so long will have gusted away into the dark November evening. We will be left with stark branches and piles of brown detritus. Jackets, scarves, gloves, sweaters, wool stockings, even long underwear will emerge from their summer hibernations. Bundled up, swaddled, we will sigh as we see our own limbs disappear under wrappings. And yet . . . and yet . . . when November actually announces itself in a whirl of flying leaves and hiss of radiators, I find I am not bereft, but expectant.

November is here with gifts a plenty. The tracery of branches outside my window lifts my spirit as much as the green of summer and the orange of fall. Squirrels race and vault along the highways of the trees. Grey days alternate with brilliant blue skies and sunshine. My jacket falls open and the sun warms my face, reminding me that there is no season without the warmth of the sun. I look out my window and the harbor, hidden all summer by the greenery, is visible again. I delight in seeing the boats, the glistening of the ocean.

My home is suddenly no longer hidden by the shade but open to the light. I revel in the comfort of coming in from the cold to a warm house. Of pumpkins and haystacks and scarecrows, and Thanksgiving on the near horizon.

A chance to sing my favorites: "Come, Ye Thankful People", "We Gather Together"—and bring into my heart again the George J. Tarr Elementary School where we sang as we colored in the pictures of the pilgrims. The memories of the smell of turkey traveling from kitchen to living room—enveloping me in a sense of well-being that is hard to recapture, but returns for a brief moment each time I get a whiff of turkey even now.

November is spare and austere, yet sparkles like champagne. November wakes us up to what we did not see in the lushness of summer and the riot of October. What do you see in November? What memories does November stir that cause you to smile, and say, yes, life still has goodness amidst the despair. Happy Thanksgiving.

In The Bleak Midwinter

"Snow had fallen, snow on snow, snow on snow, in the bleak midwinter long, long ago . . ." We heard those words of the poet Christina Georgina Rossetti at our Christmas worship, little expecting that they were to prove an accurate weather forecast for January. Prophecy at its most literal. Now we were ensconced in the bleak Wisconsin midwinter.

Snow on snow, snow on snow shovel, snow biting our faces, snow caressing our faces, snow dripping down into wool socks, snow clumping on mittens, snow grinding under our tires, snow plunging from rooftops, snow dancing under the street lights, snow to glide over on sleds and skis, snow to slip on, and we hope, snow to cushion the fall. Snow with all its accompanying joy and despair: Hurray no school. Drat, another foot of the white curse to pitch onto the pile that is growing higher and higher. Harder and harder for some of us to see snow shoveling as healthy exercise, and easier for others to admit, it was down right dangerous exercise.

We resent the extra time spent in getting in and out of the driveway morning and night, the amount of sheer work it takes just to get to work, to get food, to do the simple tasks of life we took for granted before. We plan more carefully which route is the most likely to be well plowed, which mall will provide for all our shopping needs at once. We ask is it really necessary to have pasta tonight? What is in the cupboard? Time to use those cans of soup we stored for emergencies. This is the emergency. Instead of going to bookstore or library, why not read the books that have been sitting unread in the bookcase for five years. The snowy day is here. Time to catch up on those corners of our lives we haven't had time for. Hurrah!

Snow on snow. I turn from resentment to counting my blessings for the soup, the books, for this act of nature which forces me to slow down and stay at home, to think mindfully about each task rather than zip from here to there trying to do ten hours worth of stuff in five. I learn there are many things I can actually do without—marshmallows are not essential to hot chocolate, oatmeal can replace ice cream. I may even lose that five pounds I have been promising to get disciplined about. I learn to be grateful for all the things that still work—the electricity, the phones, the heat. I come in from the storm to a cozy haven. There is a certain delight snuggling under a warm blanket watching the weather forecasters, wind whipping the snow into their eyes, report on weather conditions all over Wisconsin. Lake effect snow sounds exciting from such a perch. Yes, it is the bleak midwinter but there is a beauty in the bleakness, the white world shimmers with the iridescence of the sunlit snow. We blink awake in the strength of its light and see once again the beauty of snow on snow.

Bleak midwinters come to us throughout our lives. Sometimes they are times of great suffering, sometimes of slowing down, of living more consciously in the struggle. There is the drudgery, anguish and fear of getting through hard times. There is the other side, the iridescent, shining love that bounces back to us from the kindness of family, friends, and strangers. The peace that comes from realizing that we may be in the storm, but we are not alone. The actor Tony Perkins said that he experienced real love and kindness from the friends he met after he became ill with AIDS, a loving kindness he had never known during all the years of his Hollywood success. His bleakest midwinter revealed the iridescence of loving humanity. In the bleak midwinters of our lives, may such beauty be revealed to us. In the bleak midwinters, may we reveal that beauty to each other.

Animal Frolics

"Animal Frolics," my teacher announces softly. "First, monkey shows his claws." We students silently move our arms and hands to form the movement of the monkey showing his claws, then giving a gift. Before the sequence is over we become the crane and the bear. For two hours a week this spring I participated in a Tai Chi class in the basement of the Kenosha Public Museum. Beneath the glassy-eyed gaze of the museum's stuffed cat collection, those sad cougars and tigers who had met an untimely end so many years ago, we humans became cranes, monkeys, tigers, elephants, bears, birds, clouds and thunder, trees, guitars, archers, warriors, bell pullers, waiters.

The graceful, slow movements of Tai Chi have poetic names—Jade Maiden Threading Shuttle, Gliding Swan, Harmony. The lovely names of each exercise help to center the mind: for Tai Chi is more than exercise, it is meditation. Each movement is coordinated with breathing: breathe in as the arm goes out, breathe out as the arm comes back. Be conscious of each breath. Be conscious of each movement. Be conscious of moving slowly. Our teacher with her soft-spoken voice and her merry eyes, her gracious patience at our sometimes awkward attempts, guided us through many sequences in the two hours, each week adding another intriguing form.

Tai Chi, as exercise, fosters flexibility and balance, but it is a far cry from the high-energy, sweat-producing exercise of aerobics. Although there are some forms of Tai Chi in which the sequences are performed quickly, most Tai Chi consists of slow movements. You concentrate not on wearing yourself out but rather on perfecting each movement, on coming into harmony with your "chi" energy—the vital energy, the essence of life.

The slowness, the grace, the poetry, are all part of what I love about Tai Chi. I need the permission to go slow, to concentrate on perfection, to be consciously graceful, to be playfully imaginative. I spend much too much time running around, multi-tasking with efficiency, tensing up instead of calming down. The slowness, the grace, the constant admonitions—breathe, enjoy breathing, feel the chi, feel the life force—remind me that life needs balance, needs slow measures as well as allegros.

Tai Chi also reminds me that life needs imagination. Children play let's pretend, turning themselves into lions and tigers and bears at whim. We grow older and forget the importance of freeing our minds and bodies from the bonds of reality. In Tai Chi I take the pose of the archer and stand in Sherwood Forest, a brave and skillful Maid Marion. I am an elephant stomping, a crane in flight from a tiger, a goddess holding back a thunderstorm. I enter into a magical, mystical world, my flawed middle-aged body transformed into an instrument of grace and power.

Finally, Tai Chi reminds me that I need other people. The class moves together as a peaceful, harmonious whole. There is something that happens when we move together that simply doesn't happen when I practice alone. There is something wonderful and mysterious about being together, eight people moving as one, each different, yet each connecting through the chi we create together.

It is the same with church. I can read sermons, listen to hymns, pray and meditate alone, but there is something wonderful and mysterious about our being together, a congregation singing, praying, listening, sitting in silence, connecting through the chi we create, the Spirit of Life with us and within us. Remember that wonder and mystery, go to worship this week!

The Journey of the Manx

Never doubt that a small group of thoughtful, committed citizens can change the world; indeed it's the only thing that ever has."

Margaret Mead

These words of Margaret Mead are included in the prayerbook section of the Unitarian Universalist hymnal. The words remind us that changing the world is not a futile dream but an active possibility. That there are people who every day are in some way working together to change the world. People willing to give time, risk reputation, even sometimes their lives, to do the right thing. Extraordinary people and ordinary people, for there are so many ways, small and large, to change the world.

Sometimes we all get a bit hopeless, as we read of all the cheating, conniving, and cruelty in our world. It is then that we need to see those small groups of thoughtful people changing the world—not all at once but step by step, person to person. I got a glimpse of that hope this week when a friend sent me a news clip from the Bangor, Maine newspaper, recounting the journey of two Manx cats eleven-hundred miles from Parkersburg, West Virginia to Fredericton, New Brunswick. It took fifteen strangers to ferry the cats up north. A small group of cat-lovers linked by the website Catster, willing to be stations on the Catster Railroad.

And why? Because the two cats, a year-old mother and her four month kitten, were facing imminent euthanization. The shelter in West Virginia couldn't hold them any longer. Their prospective family had been looking for Manx cats (a breed that originated on the Isle of Man, have no tails, but do have a lively personality). The family was thrilled to finally find some Manxes, but they had no way to get to West Virginia in time to rescue the cats. It was then the shelter suggested volunteer transport through Catster.

It took a lot of e-mails and phone calls and additional help from the Maine Coon Cat Rescue and the Humane Society in Parkersburg, but the cats had a ride of a lifetime with all their conductors. The final ones were two Bangor residents who met the cats' new family in Houlton, Maine. Operation Miracle Manx was finally in the station! A small group of people changed the world for the cats and the family, giving them all new life, and for no rewards other than the satisfaction of doing good.

As I thought of these folks, others came to mind: the English men and women setting out in all sorts of boats to get to Dunkirk and rescue their soldiers, the women on an island in Denmark who raised the orphan babies diverted to their island by a storm in World War II. Many of the babies who made it to the mainland hospital died from failure to thrive syndrome, not enough loving available in the busy hospital, while the island babies flourished. The small groups in the 1960s who grew to large groups and marched their way to civil rights. The small groups meeting now in our community and throughout the world to save the world's environment, to save the world's children, to save the world.

Never doubt that a small group of committed citizens can change the world. Open your eyes and see them. Better still, join them.

A Radical "Happifying" God

A few years ago in *The New York Review of Books* in a discussion of the religious ferment in New England between the years 1790-1820, book reviewer Gordon Wood made the statement that millennial prophets and radical religious sects of all sorts emerged and flourished, "Shakers, Universalists, Free Baptists".

There we are the Universalists clearly listed among the radicals. Wood did not go on to describe just how successful those radical Universalists were at winning converts. In our Coming of Age class, however, we read about Hosea Ballou, referred to in our text as the "Father of Universalism". (This is a much-contested paternity also ascribed to both John Murray and George de Benneville. No mothers are listed, though, Judith Sargent Murray would certainly be a good choice.) I had forgotten just how successful Hosea and his fellow Universalist preachers were at evangelizing. When he converted to Universalism in 1790, it was a new denomination with approximately 5,000 members; when he died in 1852, Universalists were numbered at 800,000. This figure is astounding when we realize that today there are only 200,000 Unitarian Universalists in the United States. Even given the differences in counting methods, it has got to be a sobering statistic to those of us among the counted.

What were these radicals preaching that won so many to the fold? God loves everyone. God will save everyone from the fires of Hell. Love is the most powerful force in the world. God is one, not a trinity, with its implication that Jesus was human, not divine, and that reason should be used when reading the Bible.

Even the Unitarians of the time thought the Universalists had gone too far. The Unitarians still believed that the threat of eternal damnation was a deterrent to crime. They also looked down on the Universalists, deeming them among the great unwashed.

Hosea Ballou himself was a radical among radicals, who horrified some of the more conservative Universalists with his insistence that sin was misery here on earth and God's purpose was to free humans from sin and make them happy. He used a wonderful 18th century expression, "happify," to explain this purpose: God loves us and wants to "happify" us.

I like the idea of the happifying God, but I part ways with Ballou on another of his beliefs, God's omnipotence. I cannot reconcile a God with the power to save a person from the pain of cancer who would not do so. I can only believe that God is not all-powerful within our world. However, I do like Ballou's theology that God wants to happify us—that God simply by loving us can happify us. Perhaps not cause us to feel always jolly, as the word happify seems to imply, but at least that God's love can solace us, help us to bear the pains that not even God can take away.

All I really know of God firsthand is what I see of God reflected in other people. Those times in my life, when people have happified me with their love, those times, when my love for others has flowed from me allowing me to happify them: those are the times I have felt closest to God.

Happify—even the word brings a smile. Say it to yourself, then add: today I will try to happify someone. Think of 200,000 Unitarian Universalists happifying the world each day. Maybe we could actually win another 600,000 converts. Or maybe we could just make the world a happier place. What a radical idea!

Imagining God—A Spiritual Exercise

for Believers and Skeptics

"Praying is not necessarily best described always as looking towards God; sometimes, and especially in intercession, it is equally a learning to look at the world as if with God's eyes."
                    Rowan Williams, Archbishop of Canterbury

In my first interview for entrance into the Episcopal Divinity School, I met with a theology professor, who surprised me by saying "We create God in our imagination." Her words pleasantly shocked and liberated me. God, a product of our imagination, rather than us a product of God's! Not really so radical when you think about it, however, for God has always been the product of different human imaginations. Too often those imaginings dwell on what God is or does (particularly does for humans), who God loves and hates, what God isn't, or for atheists, that God isn't.

What strikes me about Rowan William's statement are the words: "It is equally a learning to look at the world as if with God's eyes." Shedding all the baggage of other people's imaginations, let yourself imagine what the world looks like through God's eyes . . . how the world touches God's heart. Imagine you are God looking at the world, what would you imagine yourself doing?

Would you be a superhero God zooming from hemisphere to hemisphere in rescue mode: cures for cancer, jobs, good harvests, passing grades, winning scores, zapping from your fingertips to those whose cries appealed to you? What would be your criterion for answering prayers? On what grounds would you allow a child to die in Africa and live in Sweden? Superhero God springs from the imagination of the rescued, "God saved me from the flood." But for those drowned in the flood, such a God is a colossal failure of imagination.

When I imagine looking at the world through God's eyes, with God's heart, I imagine being filled with an amazing, painful compassion, an aching heart that compels my arms to reach out to embrace the suffering world, to send steadfast, kind, healing love to everyone. Not love that kills microbes, but love that kills fear and loneliness and despair. I imagine a God who hears all prayers and can answer none with superheroics, only with compassionate love. I imagine a God who prays that we will open our hearts to receive that compassionate love, a God who aches when we answer love with hate. A God who brightens with hope when humans act with compassionate love. This is the God of my imagination, the God of the dark hours of a sleepless night and the brilliant sunshine of an October day.

How about you? Believers and skeptics, imagine the world through God's eyes. With God's heart. What God does your imagination create?

Beach Communion

As I sat on the beach this summer gazing at my grandson as he splashed, swum, socialized, and generally had a great time, I felt myself in communion with a disparate but united group—the watchers of the children. Mothers, fathers, grandparents, aunts, uncles, friends, lifeguards, conversing or meditating but always with a keen eye water-ward. For the children, our presence was all but forgotten until the goggles went missing or the ice cream truck resonated in the pines. Yet when disaster or opportunity struck, damp heads radared in on their caregiver. Little legs struggled sturdily over the sands for help or dollars.

What struck me was the faith of the children that they were being cared for, even when Mom was no longer splashing beside them in the water. Each one knew that Dad might be discussing the Red Sox, but he was looking at his child; that if one guardian had to use the rest room, another would be on duty. Even I, who knew no one else at the beach, could turn to the stranger on the next blanket and ask her to keep an eye on Alex, just as I would do for her granddaughter. No introductions were necessary. Our task was clear to each and every one of us—we were here to be sure no child was hurt or lost. We were here to ensure one more happy summer memory for a bunch of kids, only a few of whom we knew, but in that time of beach communion, all of whom we loved. We grown-ups, like the children, had faith in each other's good will.

Because of this faith, the beach was a place of noise, but calm, of high jinks but safety, of experiment but control. Each child felt free within the knowledge that if he went too far out, a voice would call him back; that if she went under, an arm would pull her up, spluttering, but otherwise unharmed. The beach was a place of grace, where all of us created a peaceable playground.

People question the presence of God in this world, not without reason in view of all the troubles on this earth; yet the presence of God is so visible if we open our eyes and hearts. Whether God is a divine spirit or God is the Human Spirit of Good in each of us. There is one representation of the goddess, Kuan Yin, with a thousand arms. She needs that many arms to do her daily work of saving the world. That is the story; the reality is that those who hold that story as their life guide, know that they must be the arms of the goddess. We too know that if the presence of God or the Spirit of Human Good is to be in the world, we must be that presence, living our lives to be a saving grace to all we meet. The joy of living in that presence is the communion we feel with the human race, with the spirit that we hold true, and the grace of being in a now in which we feel cared for, and caring.

A Miracle of Saints and Dogs

It was that season again—and I was looking, without much success, for a miracle story. Then my dog flopped down in my lap, rolled over on his belly, stuck his face into mine, and started kissing me. Obviously, he didn't want me to be thinking about miracles. He wanted some gentle pats and kind words. I patted and scratched and smiled into his button black eyes. He blissfully welcomed the full attention by snorting raucously. Then I smiled: I have a miracle right here in my lap!

I don't know what kind of dog he is. He's black with white whiskers, shaggy and softly furred, and silky when first groomed. He's twenty-five pounds and the vet's guess is that he's probably a terrier and poodle mix. But no one knows for sure, no more than we know how old he is. We know for certain that someone was cruel to him because he was found abandoned at a dump in Maine, dirty and smelly, thin and scared. What's more, he cringes and looks absolutely forlorn at any harsh word, and he barks fearfully at tall men.

He was taken from the dump to the worst dog pound in the area and put in a cell that was never cleaned: Why clean up after a dog who will be euthanized in a few days? Who would adopt a dog from this notorious pound; and if by chance anyone did come, they surely wouldn't look at this dog. The smell would drive them away, let alone his matted, grimy fur. It would take a miracle to save such a dog.

The Good Book says: Where there is great love, there are always miracles. There is a woman in Old Town, Maine. I don't know her name, but I know she is a saint. She has her very own mission. She finances it from her own pocket. Her mission is to go to the worst dog pound and rescue a dog who is slated to die that day. She can't do it every day, but she does it as often as she can.

So one day, she took that grimy, stinking dog out of his cell and drove him to her vet. That was Miracle Number One for the dog. When she got to the vet, the assistants took one look and one whiff and pooled their money to pay for the dog's grooming: Miracle Number Two. Then this saintly woman paid for the dog's board and put an ad in the paper offering him for sale. She always puts a price on the dogs because she wants to be certain people are serious about caring for a dog. She adjusts the price according to circumstances. So the dog was clean and well-fed, and people were being kind to him: Miracle Number Three.

But the dog was still homeless. Meanwhile my son and I were grieving because we had tried to work a miracle and failed. We had paid a lot of money and traveled far for an operation for our wire-haired terrier puppy, Beastie, but the operation had failed. He'd been given two years to live, and just that week he had died. There had been the chance that perhaps the doctors were wrong, and that love and faith could have given him a natural life span; but love wasn't enough. Still he'd had a happy home and he'd never known he was under a death sentence. He'd never cringed or gone hungry or been left in the cold. The night he was dying I'd slept on the floor beside him. He hadn't been alone, dirty, hungry, or unloved; and he'd lived a full two years. Maybe that was the miracle.

We were looking for a new dog. We'd gone to the good pounds, but the dogs were too big. I couldn't afford another purebred. Then I read the saint's ad: Terrier/Poodle for sale.

"That could mean an Airedale and a full-size poodle," I said to my son.

"Answer the ad, Mother," he replied.

Miracle Number Four for the dog: a son who knew what his mother needed. The new dog was at our vet's. The same veterinary assistant who had held me as I cried a few days before met me with a smile: "Oh, this dog would be wonderful for you. He's such a sweet dog," she said.

"Just tell me one thing before I see him: Is his heart all right?" I asked.

"His heart is fine."

We were supposed to keep him for the weekend and decide. By the time we'd walked him home we knew. Miracle Number Five: the dog had found a home. He was a quiet dog on that first walk, not like our adventurous terrier. He'd been named Timmy at the vet's because he was so timid. After the first fifteen minutes in our house, I asked my son, "What shall we name him?"

"Cheech," he replied, after his favorite outrageous comedian.

"Cheech," I said. "We'll make him cheeky yet."

Miracle Number Six, we did.

When I think of Cheech's story, I know there are miracles: that even for the absolutely hopeless there is hope. For there are saints in this world. Saints who don't get in the books or win prizes, but saints who change lives and work miracles.

This particular saint made a little dog whole again. She made my life and my son's life whole again. She even made some sense out of our other dog's death, for it seemed that because it had to happen, wasn't it a miracle that it happened then? And this saint, this woman, keeps doing this, quietly, on her own, she saves animals and heals broken hearts. This woman is a miracle herself in a world that is so dark that animals are thrown on garbage heaps. When I think of her, I feel humbled, and I also feel God's presence and I know in my own heart what is meant by the miracle of redeeming love.

When Hope is Hard to Find

"And I'll bring you hope when hope is hard to find . . ." So goes the refrain of one of my favorite hymns, *"Come, Sing a Song with Me"* by Carolyn McDade.

It is a big promise—bringing hope when hope is hard to find. Is it really possible to do so? Can one person bring another hope, especially in situations that seem ultimately hopeless? Into my mind flashes the image of two people falling from the Twin Towers hand in hand. Beyond hope . . . yet to hold hands with a friend in that most terrifying moment between life and death is an act of hope, the final affirmation of love, the gift given to each other, that they would not die alone, but go hand in hand into eternity. They were present for each other, giving each other hope, even unto the end.

When my grandmother had a stroke that paralyzed her, she was terrified of going to the hospital. For her, hospitalization meant being left alone to die. Knowing her fear, my mother with the help of her sisters nursed my grandmother at home for the six months before she died. My grandmother couldn't speak, but she could hear and see and feel. Her bedroom became the place for her grandchildren to check in after school, the place for her daughters to sit quietly, to read to her, to tell her of the events of their day—to bring her hope amidst the hopelessness. Nothing could cure her, but the presence of those she loved was healing, the fear of abandonment left her eyes. I remember standing on a table to show her my new ballet costume. Her eyes lit up. She almost managed to smile. The presence of her family brought my grandmother hope. Their presence turned her dying days into living days. They gave her hope when hope was hard to find.

There are times in our lives when we suffer terrible disappointments and heartrending losses, debilitating physical illness or mental depressions. Others cannot take away our grief or rescue us from our situation. Yet they can be there with us. We do not have to be alone. We can accept their loving presence, just as we can be a loving presence for others when our lives are once more righted. The hope that is hard to find is the simple hope of the hand extended to help, the knowledge that we are not alone with our pain but surrounded by the presence of friends—the hope of their love

There are times when the only hope we can offer each other is our loving presence. No matter how painful life becomes, how close death looms, remember the hope of your presence. Be that hope for each other when hope is hard to find.